STRAVINSKY

MUSICOLOGY: A BOOK SERIES
Edited by F. Joseph Smith

STRAVINSKY
The Music Box and the Nightingale

Daniel Albright

University of Rochester

Gordon and Breach

New York   London   Paris   Montreux   Tokyo   Melbourne

Gordon and Breach Science Publishers

Post Office Box 786
Cooper Station
New York, New York 10276
United States of America

Post Office Box 197
London WC2E 9PX
United Kingdom

58, rue Lhomond
75005 Paris
France

Post Office Box 161
1820 Montreux 2
Switzerland

3-14-9, Okubo
Shinjuku-ku, Tokyo 169
Japan

Private Bag 8
Camberwell, Victoria 3124
Australia

Library of Congress Cataloging-in-Publication Data

Albright, Daniel, 1945-
  Stravinsky : the music box and the nightingale / Daniel Albright.
    p.   cm. — (Musicology, ISSN 0275-5866 : v. 9)
  Bibliography: p.
  Includes index.
  ISBN 2-88124-295-2
  1. Stravinsky, Igor, 1882-1971—Criticism and interpretation.
I. Title. II. Series: Musicology (New York, N.Y.) : v. 9.
ML410.S932A6 1988   L8 714
780'.92'4—dc19   88-16380
                                             CIP
                                             MN

Cover photo: Hogarth, *A Rake's Progress* III: The Orgy

CONTENTS

INTRODUCTION TO THE SERIES

The Gordon and Breach *Musicology* series, a companion to the *Journal of Musicological Research*, covers a creative range of musical topics, from historical and theoretical subjects to social and philosophical studies. Volumes thus far published show the extent of this broad spectrum, from *Music and Its Social Meanings, Music from the Middle Ages through the Twentieth Century: Essays in Honor of Gwynn S. McPeek*, and *Understanding the Musical Experience*, to the present volume, *Stravinsky: The Music Box and the Nightingale*. The editor also welcomes interdisciplinary studies, ethnomusicological works, and performance analyses. With this series, it is our aim to expand the field and definition of musical exploration and research.

I.

The Unnaturalness of Nature

What is Stravinsky's music about? There are several ways of answering that question. The critic can say that a piece of Stravinsky's is about how rhythm governs the tension between certain melodic intervals. Stravinsky had no objection to this approach. But the critic always wants to say more, and then he gets into trouble.

Music criticism, like the criticism of painting and of literature, consists of the struggle to remove an object from the world in which it takes place (the Amsterdam Concertgebouw, the Louvre, the shelf of my library) and to deposit it somewhere else. I might deposit a musical composition on a mathematical grid to study pitches and meters; or I might deposit it amid similar musical compositions to note its deviations from some theoretical norm. But if I feel tempted to deposit it outside, in the world of experience, and to relate its intelligible sounds to the birdcalls, whistles, thunders, automobile traffic, shouts, I have, according to Stravinsky, committed a hostile act.

Stravinsky went to great pains to deny that music had any significant relation to the outer world—or to the inner one. In his first major statement of aesthetics, in 1936, he wrote the most often quoted sentence of his life:

> For I consider that music is, by its very nature, essentially powerless to *express* anything at all, whether a feeling, an attitude of mind, a psychological mood, a phenomenon of nature, etc. . . . . *Expression* has never been an inherent property of music. . . . If, as is nearly always the case, music appears to express something, this is only an illusion and not a reality. It is simply an additional attribute which, by tacit and inveterate agreement, we have lent it, thrust upon it, as a label, a convention . . . (*An Autobiography,* pp. 53-54)

If there is an expressive aspect to music, that aspect has simply been tied to the helpless notes like a tin can to a dog's tail. We fasten the expressiveness to the piece of music, and then pull it up and admire it as if it were a new discovery. In later life Stravinsky tried to clarify this remark:

> The over-publicized bit about expression (or non-expression) was simply a way of saying that music is supra-personal and super-real and as such beyond verbal meanings and verbal descriptions. . . . It was offhand and annoyingly incomplete, but even the stupider critics could have seen that it did not deny musical expressivity, but only the validity of a type of verbal statement about musical expressivity. I stand by the remark, incidentally, though today I would put it the other way around: music expresses itself. (*Expositions and Developments*, p. 101)

This formula, however, leaves the critic as disabled as before. The critic has only his vocabulary, which he knows to be crude and inept when confronting the non-verbal, and yet which he hopes can clasp something of the music it reaches toward. But if music is supra-personal and super-real, it inhabits its own crystaline sphere beyond the range of verbal apprehension, an object that can never be hauled down into the critic's homely universe of discourse. Stravinsky simply laughs at the critic who thinks that Liszt's *Nuages gris* was caused by gray clouds (*Conversations with Igor Stravinsky*, p. 19); indeed, "The one true comment on a piece of music is another piece of music" (*Dialogues*, p. 63). It is easy to accept that no essay could take the place of *The Rite of Spring*; and yet, it is doubtful that language is wholly useless at criticizing music. If it were, Stravinsky himself wasted many an hour at this vain job.

Despite all this certitude about music's immiscibility with the natural world and with discourse, a study of Stravinsky's remarks shows a surprising amount of leakage. Whether or not Liszt had ever observed a gray cloud before writing *Gray Clouds*, Stravinsky knew of an occasion when he himself wrote a piece of music in direct response to an outer stimulus: the second of his *Three Pieces for String Quartet* (1915), developed from the "jerky, spastic movement" of a clown called Little Tich (*Memories and Commentaries*, p. 95). Similarly, though Stravinsky hated imitative effects, hated the notion of music as illustrator or mood-creator or handmaid to some other art, he nevertheless pointed out a few bits of mimesis among his own compositions: for instance, a passage in his *Symphony of Psalms* where triplets for horn and piano suggest Elijah's chariot ascending to heaven (*D* 46). At least momentarily, music can find itself embedded in a larger, lower world, and without too much contamination from the verbal, pictorial, and human company in which it finds itself.

But it is also possible that music can be "about" something in much more global ways. After 1966, when Stravinsky was eighty-four years old, he found himself too weak to compose; and he spent much of his time listening to Beethoven on the phonograph. In youth and middle age, Stravinsky had on occasion found Beethoven-bashing a pleasant pastime; but at the end of his life he found himself engaged in an increasingly intimate and rewarding study of his music. And he wanted to find a kind of meaning in the music, although he could state it only in a gingerly fashion:

> Does a world of the Beethoven quartets exist outside of music, then, and is it possible to discover a reflective system between the language structure of the music and the structure of the phenomenal world? No, to the first, but to the second, well, yes, perhaps, eventually. . . . My . . . belief is that the quartets are a charter of human rights . . . A high concept of freedom *is* embodied in the quartets, both beyond and including what Beethoven himself meant when he wrote to Prince Galitzin that his music could "help suffering mankind." (*Themes and Conclusions*, p. 147)

Here Stravinsky did not retreat from his insistence on the autonomy of the musical act—it is not contingent on or expressive of something outside itself. But, by positing a "reflective system" between music and the world of experience, he liberated music from the narcissism that threatened it when it could express only itself, when it seemed to disdain contact with the mire of organic life. Beethoven's quartets may not be free; they may not be an expression of freedom; but there is something about their cobbling-together that is analogous to what freedom is in human life. Stravinsky was never moved by the choral finale to Beethoven's Ninth Symphony, which he thought a hopelessly banal tune affixed to Schiller's mighty ode of liberation and brotherhood; but the late quartets, with their sophisticated upheaval of sonata-form, seemed a mirror-image of political freedom. Music, then, can be "about" freedom, not by setting a text urging men to be free, but through its own internal constitutive processes.

There are few other examples from Stravinsky's published writings of reflections between music and the phenomenal world. Indeed, he seemed to believe that music criticism did not yet exist but might some day exist, "well, yes, perhaps, eventually." And, although he busied himself a little with music criticism, he did not write formal essays—he only threw out speculations, usually in the course of dialogues with Robert Craft. There is scarcely a single word of Stravinsky's that can be attributed to him with perfect confidence, except in his letters—otherwise his published works are hybrids or fakes. Among his chief literary co-workers were Roland-Manuel (the author of "Stravinsky"'s *Poetics of Music*—he also helped with the writing of *An Autobiography*) and Robert Craft. (So reticent was Stravinsky about unmediated appearance on paper that he would occasionally sign letters, ''Robert Craft,'' even when he wrote them himself.) Therefore his criticism, like Socrates', is a record of a mind in flight, never pausing to chisel an argument into final form. He did not close, tighten, or fully define his discourse. As he himself said, referring to the grammatical form of his name in Russian, I am an adjective, not a noun (*TC* 32).

If Beethoven's music is ''about'' freedom, what is Stravinsky's ''about''? I am tempted to say *slavery*, so much did he insist on the strictness and rigidity of his processes of composition, on the exactitude of metronome markings, on *secco* textures and inflexible rhythms. But there is another, I think better, argument to be made.

In old age Stravinsky frequently found himself defending his decision to become a serial (or twelve-tone) composer—that is, to write music not in major or minor keys based on a fundamental note, but in a system where each of the twelve notes of the chromatic scale has equal importance. Many listeners found his serial music discordant or disorienting, dry, distant, wholly different from the opulent popular successes of his early period, such as *The Firebird*. Stravinsky thought that those who disliked serial music for its harsh, mathematical character made a serious error in thinking that the old, major-minor tonal system (on which is based everything from *Jingle Bells* to Wagner's *Götterdämmerung*) is somehow ''natural'':

> . . . yesterday's non-starter [the man who resists serial music] . . . opposed the substitution of an ''arbitrary order'' (those Draconian twelve-tone laws!) for a ''natural gravitational system,'' as if both the arbitrary and the natural were not equally artificial and composed. (*TC* 92)

This, I think, is what Stravinsky's music is ''about'': the deep equivalence of the natural and the artificial. At the center of his dramatic imagination is the desire to juxtapose in a single work two competing systems—one of which seems natural, tasteful, approved alike by man and God, the other of which seems artificial, abhorrent, devilish—and to subvert these distinctions as best he can.

A certain anxiety about the unnaturalness of nature is an old theme in nineteenth-century art. Heinrich von Kleist, in his dialogue-essay ''On the Puppet Theater'' (1810) had one of his characters claim that every ballerina tries in vain to imitate the perfect grace of marionettes, whose limbs, moved by a system of counterweighted pendulums, trace a precision of gesture impossible to mere human flesh. Kleist even drew a comparison between the puppet and the god:

"—But just as two intersecting lines, converging on one side of a point, reappear on the other after their passage through infinity, and just as our image, as we approach a concave mirror, vanishes to infinity only to reappear before our very eyes, so will grace, having likewise traversed the infinite, return to us once more, and so appear most purely in that bodily form that has either no consciousness at all or an infinite one, which is to say, either in the puppet or a god."

"That means," said I, somewhat amused, "that we would have to eat of the tree of knowledge a second time to fall back into the state of innocence."

"Of course," he answered, "and that is the final chapter in the history of the world."

This state of envy for the inorganic would grow more common as the century progressed. E. T. A. Hoffmann, the German writer of fantastic tales, found his best shock-effects in the confusions between dead images and living organisms—shadows and mirror-reflections that embody human souls, paintings that come to life, the toy nutcracker that springs up to do battle with a mouse. Among the most resonant of his tales was "Der Sandmann" (1817) in which a man, looking through a distorting lens, falls in love with a lifesized mechanical woman, the "daughter" of one of his professors; he meets her at her coming-out party, where the precision of her dancing puts other dancers to shame, and her singing is "almost too sharp, but clear as glass bells":

> So, without being observed, he took Coppola's glass out of his pocket, and directed it upon the beautiful Olimpia. Oh! then he perceived how her yearning eyes sought him, how every note only reached its full purity in the loving glance which penetrated to and inflamed his heart. Her artificial *roulades* seemed to him to be the exultant cry towards heaven of the soul refined by love; and when at last, after the *cadenza*, the long trill rang shrilly and loudly through the hall, he felt as if he were suddenly grasped by burning arms and could no longer control himself . . . (*Weird Tales*, translated by J. T. Bealby, volume I, p. 201)

After much wooing and long humiliation, this romantical fellow learns that his darling is not human. Both before and after this revelation, however, he is subject to fits and dreams, during which Clara—his hometown, organic sweetheart, a sensible girl—seems to look like an automaton; the wall of separation between person and thing is unstable, shifting.

What is interesting, for our purposes, is that the "expressiveness" of Olympia's aria is of exactly the style that Stravinsky reported in *An Autobiography*: the exultation of her cry, evidence of a "soul refined by love," is simply superadded by the listener; her song is pure music, objective and

soulless. Hoffmann was a professional composer and music-critic as well as a short-story writer, and some suspicion of the unreality of romantic expressivity seems to have dwelt in this most romantic of tale-tellers. Elsewhere, too, Hoffmann considered the dangerousness of expression; for instance, his story "Rath Krespel" tells of an invalid soprano forbidden to sing, but whose need to express herself is so urgent that she sings herself to death. In a strange way Hoffmann seems to recommend apathy, the life of the automaton; though he may also have felt some sympathy with those university boys at the end of "Der Sandmann" who look for small errors in the singing and dancing of their girlfriends, endearing imperfections that prove them made of flesh and blood.

The prestige of Hoffmann's tales among musicians and artists has always been great. "Der Sandmann" was the basis of Delibes's ballet *Coppélia* (1870), of one act (and "Rath Krespel" the basis of another) of Offenbach's *Les Contes d'Hoffmann* (1881), and of an episode in Fellini's film *Casanova* (1976). "Der Sandmann," like Kleist's essay, is disturbing because it suggests the morbidity of the ideal. Plato taught that ideal forms are beyond our life, unsusceptible to the taint of dirt, knowable only through copies; but, by the nineteenth century, as the art of modeling grew more cunning, certain contrivances of metal, wood, paint, glass, seemed capable of embodying the ideal directly, imperishably, as if we could hope to embrace not a woman but Woman itself. Olympia, the ideally beautiful doll, is a goddess reduced to a puppet-parody—the penultimate chapter of the world's history.

"Der Sandmann" helped to teach the world that the highest sort of art might inhabit a dubious limbo between life and death. In the ballet, particularly, the boundary-line became uncertain. Two of the greatest ballets of the nineteenth century are *Coppélia* and Adam's *Giselle* (1841): one is the story of a dancer who pretends to be the faultless machine with whom her sweetheart has fallen in love; the other is the story of a man whom the spirits of unmarried maidens—the Wilis—compel to dance himself to death. The first tells of a dead thing that lifts itself into a semblance of life, and of a woman who substitutes herself for the surrogate; the second tells of a live dancer transported into such rapture of movement that he dies. The dancer, then, dances on the knife-edge between life and death, looking from one side like ecstatic flesh, on the other side like a machine or a corpse. At the peak of the dance, the perfection of nature and the perfection of unnature converge, seem ready to trade places, as in the image in the concave mirror of Kleist's simile.

W. B. Yeats, who was sensitive to these traditions, and who knew all about puppets that look like gods, suggests something of this mysterious equivalence in his poem ''The Double Vision of Michael Robartes'' (1919). The first of the two visions mentioned in the title shows mankind in a condition of total extinction, a lump of dough pounded by a puppet-demiurge until it regains a human shape:

> *Under blank eyes and fingers never still*
> *The particular is pounded till it is man.*
> *When had I my own will?*
> *O not since life began.*
>
> *Constrained, arraigned, baffled, bent and unbent*
> *By these wire-jointed jaws and limbs of wood . . .*

In the second vision, the poet leaps from self-surrender to its opposite, a blaze of exaltation:

> *On the grey rock of Cashel I suddenly saw*
> *A Sphinx with woman breast and lion paw,*
> *A Buddha, hand at rest,*
> *Hand lifted up that blest;*
>
> *And right between these two a girl at play*
> *That, it may be, had danced her life away,*
> *For now being dead it seemed*
> *That she of dancing dreamed. . . .*
>
> *In contemplation had those three so wrought*
> *Upon a moment, and so stretched it out*
> *That they, time overthrown,*
> *Were dead yet flesh and bone.*
>
> (Variorum Edition, pp. 383-84)

In this unearthly landscape, dancing between the Sphinx (symbol of the triumphant intellect, introspective and self-united) and the Buddha (symbol of the pathetic, desiring mind, looking outward), Yeats's girl supersedes all the fractures and dissociations of the world of experience: she is a thinking body, at once quick and dead, the still point of her own private turning world, a translunar Coppélia. In the dance artifice and nature are most intimate, as if each were the culmination of the other.

II.

Petrushka: The Ghost and the Machine

Stravinsky achieved international fame as a composer of ballet, with *The Firebird* (1910), *Petrushka* (1911), and *The Rite of Spring* (1913). In later life he expressed surprise that he could have made a career in ballet, in an era when ballet seemed slightly fatuous and outmoded; but the genre of dance suited his favorite themes perfectly. The plot of *The Firebird* never attracted Stravinsky greatly (*ED* 128); but the two later ballets were perfectly designed to show off the Giselle-Coppélia theme, the contact-line between human being and eidolon or corpse.

Petrushka began its existence not as a ballet but as a kind of piano concerto:

> My first idea was to compose a *Konzertstück*, a sort of combat between the piano and the orchestra. . . . In that first version I saw a man in evening dress, with long hair, the musician or poet of romantic tradition. He placed several heteroclite objects on the keyboard and rolled them up and down. At this the orchestra exploded with the most vehement protestations—hammer blows, in fact. . . . (Vera Stravinsky and Robert Craft, *Stravinsky in Pictures and Documents*, p. 66)

Here we have objects that speak, by rolling on the piano keys; and a hammer in the orchestra that replies. (In the finished ballet, this effect is most clearly heard near the beginning of the Second Tableau—the first music Stravinsky wrote for the score—in which a piano cadenza, all black keys in the left hand, all white keys in the right hand, introduces an orchestral caterwaul

representing Petrushka's curses. This cadenza gives a credible imitation of
a bowling-ball studded with nails, thrown around the keyboard.) The character of Petrushka, the puppet given life by a Charlatan, is one of these talk-
ing objects promoted into the role of doll. Petrushka, that "droll, ugly,
sentimental, shifting personage" (*PD* 67), is paradoxically the most human
creature in the entire ballet. Stravinsky seems able to attribute pathos, de-
jection, jealousy, wit more easily to an object than to a man. Things have
passions, while the real people at the carnival behave obtusely, coarsely.

The ballet tells the story of Petrushka, the Ballerina, and the Moor, three
puppets whom the Charlatan invests with life so that their dances may
amuse the visitors at the Shrove-tide fair. Petrushka falls in love with the
Ballerina, who only scorns his deformity; she prefers the attentions of the
Moor. Petrushka, mad with jealousy, interrupts the two lovers; the Moor
runs after him and kills him with his scimitar. The crowd is horrified—until
the Charlatan shows them that Petrushka is only a doll filled with sawdust.
But on the rooftop Petrushka's spirit appears, waving his arms, mocking,
threatening.

The music of *Petrushka* depends on the contrasts among three different
clusters of characters: 1) the crowd, rambunctious, loud, stomping, earthy,
often accompanied by music derived from folk themes; 2) the Ballerina and
the Moor, whose music is simple, repetitive, "balletic" in a dim, Minkus-
like, rehearsal-piano style; and 3) Petrushka himself, by turns furious,
grumpy, abrupt—his emotions are portrayed with the full resources of modern expressive dissonance, a style flexible in rhythm and harmony. The two
classes of puppet-music show two different strategies for escaping from the
aesthetic of expressionism: Petrushka's music parodies expression, while
the Ballerina remains purely inexpressive, a stick figure moving (in the
"Danse de la Ballerine") stiffly, metronomically, to inflectionless cornet ar-
peggios—she is an object, and deserves "objective" music.

Toward the beginning of *Petrushka* a music-box plays a little tune; and
melodies appropriate to music-boxes are common throughout the ballet. The

ТАНЕЦЪ БАЛЕРИНЫ.
(СЪ КОРНЕТЪ-А-ПИСТОНОМЪ ВЪ РУКАХЪ).

DANSE DE LA BALERINE.
(CORNET-À-PISTONS À LA MAIN.)

spell that breathes life into the puppets is a flute tune, played by the Charlatan, called the "Tour de Passe-passe," a section that Debussy commended
for its "sonorous magic" (*C* 48); the pan-pipe-like melody zooms up and
down and up and down in eccentric triads. It is a sort of snake-charmer tune;
its mechanical nature may hint that the wooden puppets brought to life will
in fact remain wood, tapping their feet to the Charlatan's bidding.

Stravinsky wrote that he imagined the Charlatan as "a character out of
Hoffmann . . . the flute music, too, is Weber-like, or Hoffmann-like" (*MC*
33-34). Now in Offenbach's *Les Contes d'Hoffmann* the aria of the doll
Olympia is a piece of flute-like coloratura, in which one hears all too literally the tension on the mainspring of her wind-up voicebox. Stravinsky
has converted Hoffmann's mechanical doll from a figure of fun into a figure
of power. *Petrushka* is "Der Sandmann" told from the doll's point of view,
a fable about insensitive human beings unable to appreciate the energy and
precision of a puppet. At the end Petrushka derides not only the crowd at the
carnival, but us, the spectators of the ballet, as well:

> Petroushka's ghost, as I conceived the story, is the real Petroushka, and his
> appearance at the end makes the Petrushka of the preceding play a mere doll.
> His gesture is not one of triumph or protest, as is often said, but a nose-
> thumbing addressed to the audience. (*MC* 34)

The most vital spirits are those that incarnate themselves in things. *Petrushka* is a ballet about abstract forces, forces that never descend into human beings, but that may electrify objects temporarily. It is (at least in
retrospect) a parable about the objectivity of music, for music pertains not
to the passions of men, but to something supra-personal, super-real—the
human subject is carved up into a ghost and a doll. It is Stravinsky's first
attempt to create a theatre of speaking, singing, dancing objects, to realize
on stage his vision of an objective music cut free from the slush of expression. The only expressive "subject" in the ballet is filled with sawdust, and
twists his pliant limbs in an impudent semblance of emotion.

Two trumpets play the music that accompanies this nose-thumbing: they wander off into different, extremely remote keys—C major and F# major—and, oblivious of the clash, keep playing. (The superimposition of these two keys is Petrushka's harmonic signature throughout the ballet.) This striking effect suggests how far afield from the conventions of common, affable musical discourse Stravinsky is willing to go: Petrushka, like the music itself, ends by inhabiting a different world, at right angles to the world of the spectators at the carnival.

It was Stravinsky's peculiar gift that he could write stage-pieces that represent simultaneously the extreme concreteness and the extreme abstraction of music, as he understood it. The end of *Petrushka* dismisses the whole fable; if Stravinsky had specified that the ghost of Petrushka was deriding the fairgoers from the planet Pluto he could not have produced a greater impression of remoteness, unearthliness. (The equivalent moment in Schoenberg's work occurred in 1908, in his Second Quartet, when a soprano sings—just before the music abandons any semblance of a key signature—"I feel air from another planet.") The ballet unballetizes itself, turns back into abstract music. What began as a *Konzertstück* for piano ends as exactly that.

In many places in his writings, Stravinsky affirmed the essentially abstract character of music: for instance, he claimed that *musique concrète*—music made of arranged noises rather than sounds produced by musical instruments—fails because it violates the "transcendent (or 'abstract' or 'self-contained') nature of music" (*TC* 188). And yet, Stravinsky regarded musical compositions as objects, and spoke of composing as a craft akin to the construction of a chair. Even musical intervals were, in a sense, things:

> After working late one night I retired to bed still troubled by an interval. I dreamed about this interval. It had become an elastic substance stretching exactly between the two notes I had composed, but underneath these notes at either end was an egg, a large testicular egg. The eggs were gelatinous to the touch (I touched them) . . . I woke up knowing that my interval was right. (*C* 17-18)

The fables that most attracted Stravinsky were those that let him express the inexpressiveness of music—its abstraction from human passions—and the objectivity of music—its constitution of its own world of things. Therefore he liked puppets, liked machines, liked musical-instrument stage-props (such as the Goat's *guzla* in *Renard*, the Devil's violin in *The Soldier's Tale*, or, in *Orpheus*, the lyre that lives on, even after Orpheus' death). The stage-pieces continually work to stifle, suppress the human subject, as if musical instruments and tangible note-intervals, dangling down in their own private space, were glad to be rid of those who played them.

III.

The Rite of Spring: The Prehistoric and the Posthistoric

After *Petrushka*, Stravinsky's next work was *The Rite of Spring*. Here, it seems, we are as far as possible from the mechanical or the doll-like: the action of this ballet takes place in pagan Russia, and shows the wakening of the earth from winter, the ceremonial games and conjurings of spring, and at last the sacrifice of a virgin to the Nature-god. One might argue that Stravinsky's music, instead of being inexpressive, is in fact all-expressive: for in its ferocity, its driving rhythms, it seeks to embody the trembling, the heaving, the spurting, the huge sexuality of Nature itself. As the original libretto itself says, the ballet is not a story but a surge (*PD* 75).

And yet, *The Rite of Spring* is, in its way, as distant from finite human expression as *Petrushka* is. It represents a convergence of the all-expressive with the non-expressive, a coincidence of opposites. Human subjects dwindle, disappear before the Nature-fury that animates them.

Most of the documents that survive from the ballet's inception suggest that all its collaborators were aware of the anti-human tendencies of *The Rite of Spring*. The libretto was written by Stravinsky and Nicolas Roerich (who also designed the set); an early letter by Roerich shows that he planned to dress the men "in bearskins, to show that the bear was man's ancestor" (*PD* 77). This suggests that the subject of the ballet consisted of men so primitive that they were themselves half-bears—it would have been only one step to a spectacle (like Stravinsky's *Renard*) in which the actors were themselves animals. Nijinsky, the ballet's choreographer, said in an interview in 1913—the year of the première—that "It is really the soul of nature expressed by movement to music. It is the life of the stones and the trees. There are no human beings in it'' (*PD* 95). And Stravinsky himself, in an essay published in *Montjoie!* (1913)—the text of which is even more dubious than most Stravinsky texts—offered, or may have offered, these comments:

> . . . I have tried to express in this Prelude the fear of nature before the arising of beauty, a sacred terror at the midday sun . . . some adolescent boys appear with a very old woman, whose age and even whose century is unknown, who knows the secrets of nature . . . She runs, bent over the earth, half-woman, half-beast . . . the adolescent girls come from the river. . . . They are not entirely formed beings; their sex is single and double . . . The Elect [the sacrificial virgin] is she whom the Spring is to consecrate, and who will give back to Spring the force that youth has taken from it. . . . The annual cycle of forces which are born again, and which fall again into the bosom of nature, is accomplished in its essential rhythms. (*PD* 525)

The Rite of Spring, then, concerns the human race before it has become human, before sexual differentiation, when it is still only a provisional manifestation of Nature. Men and women arise laboriously out of the earth, lumpish and half-formed, and at last subside back into it. Petrushka, like any doll, is post-human, an artifact derived from human shape; *The Rite of Spring* depicts the pre-human. It is strange that Stravinsky despised Disney's cartoon of this ballet, in *Fantasia* (1940)—Stravinsky called it an ''unresisting imbecility'' (*ED* 146)—for by making the action a minuet of dinosaurs and volcanos Disney succeeded in eliminating the human presences that were always to some extent an embarrassment to the spectacle.

The Rite of Spring represents another version of the assault on subjectivity that is part of Stravinsky's program for objectifying music. We know that the origin of the ballet was a vision of death:

> One day, when I was finishing the last pages of *L'Oiseau de Feu* in St. Petersburg, I had a fleeting vision which came to me as a complete surprise . . . I saw in imagination a solemn pagan rite: sage elders, seated in a circle, watched a young girl dance herself to death. (*A* 31)

If *Petrushka* is a new *Coppélia*, *The Rite of Spring* is a new *Giselle*. (*The Soldier's Tale* also contains a *Giselle*-episode, in which the soldier plays on his violin a tune that compels the devil to dance until he collapses in exhaustion.) Dancing is an act that pertains to death, or at least to energies that are beyond the merely human. Not only the girl of the sacrifice, but all the characters of the ballet are effaced, dehumanized, by the obliterating music of Stravinsky's score. It has proved to be almost undanceable: no choreographer has yet designed human movement that derives intelligibly from the rhythmic impulse of the music (Paul Taylor's cheeky setting of the two-piano version perhaps comes closest); and Stravinsky himself came to prefer to hear it in the concert hall, instead of the theatre. At the première, the most famous fiasco in the history of music, Nijinsky told the dancers to pay no attention to the conductor or to the music, but rather to coordinate their gestures according to a cadence that he, Nijinsky, counted out backstage; but the dancers were unable to follow even this simplified beat (*ED* 143). The drum-beats and brass chords pound the human agents back to clay; no subject can sustain itself before that onslaught of force.

The Rite of Spring is the climax of Nature-expression; but in it there are also hints of the unnatural as well. When T. S. Eliot heard it in 1921 he wrote that the music seemed to "transform the rhythm of the steppes into the scream of the motor-horn, the rattle of machinery, the grind of wheels, the beating of iron and steel, the roar of the underground railway, and the other barbaric noises of modern life" (Lyndall Gordon, *Eliot's Early Years*, p. 108). Similarly, Jean Cocteau called the Dance of the Chosen One "a mad, naive dance, dance of an insect, of a doe fascinated by a boa, of a factory blowing up" (Lederman, *Stravinsky in the Theatre*, p. 18). It is easy for any hearer, I think, to transpose the scene of the libretto—a bare spring landscape depopulated except for some small bear-like men—into another scene entirely: a bare urban landscape populated entirely by heavy-industrial machines. The post-human vista is latent in the music; and I would enjoy seeing a production of the ballet that took its staging from Eliot's comment.

However, the most unnatural re-imagining of *The Rite of Spring* comes not from Eliot but from Thomas Pynchon, in his novel *V.* (1963). This is the story of a woman of many identities, V., the agent of every political catastrophe of the twentieth century, and also the spirit of artistic Modernism. At every stage of her sinister career she substitutes prostheses for various limbs (a glass eye with a little clock in it, an ivory foot with the veins in intaglio instead of bas-relief), so that as she ages she turns increasingly beautiful and inorganic—she is a Clara determined to become Olympia by cultivating soullessness. The year 1913—the year of the première of *The Rite of Spring*—finds her in Paris as a Lesbian fetishist in love with a ballerina, Mélanie, from a company clearly modeled on Diaghilev's *Ballets Russes*. V. devotes herself to increasingly dangerous objectifications of herself and her ballerina lover; her only desire is to turn them both into things:

> It was a variation on . . . the Tristan-and-Iseult theme . . . "the act of love and the act of death are one." Dead at last, they would be one with the in-

animate universe and with each other. Love-play until then thus becomes an impersonation of the inanimate, a transvestism not between sexes but between quick and dead; human and fetish. (p. 385)

Mélanie is to dance the lead role in a new ballet called *The Rape of the Chinese Virgins*, in which she plays a virgin tortured to death defending her purity against the invading Mongols. All the other female parts are taken by dancing automata, built by a German engineer. At the end at the ballet, she is to be impaled by the Mongols; but, at the première, she neglects to put on the protective chastity belt into which the tip of the pole is to fit, so that she is really killed on stage. (It is possible that Pynchon got the impalement theme from Chabrier's *L'Étoile* [1877], in which a gorgeous impalement-device figures in the Act I finale.)

Pynchon's revised *The Rite of Spring* skillfully adds the *Coppélia* theme to the *Giselle* theme of Stravinsky's original: the dancers are demoted to wind-up toys, except for the heroine, who yearns to join them in inanimation. I think that Pynchon was right to understand that *The Rite of Spring*, like other works of Stravinsky, treats the sexuality of objects, the erotics of death. Recent scholarship has defined the fetish in contrast to the idol:

> [Idolatry] preserves a residual consciousness that what is worshipped is only represented by, not embodied in, the idol; fetishism is a step further down the ladder in that it worships things as and for themselves. (David Simpson, *Fetishism and Imagination*, p. 13).

In the fetish we have an extremely primitive religion as well as a decadent sexuality—the convergence of the sophisticated and the prehistoric.

Stravinsky's investment of a object-world with human passion, more-than-human passion, leads properly to Pynchon's substitution of automata for human dancers. The world of Stravinsky's music is a domain of super-saturated objects, where human affections have been translated, transubstantiated, into something alien:

> If a movement in a ballet should happen to be a visualization of the words "I Love You," then this reference to the actual world would play the same role in the dance that a guitar would play in a Picasso still-life: something of the real world is caught as pretext or clothing for the inherent abstraction. . . . Even in older ballets like *Giselle*, descriptiveness has been removed . . . to a level of objectivity and pure art-play. (*PD* 358)

In *Giselle*, the deathliness of art is an explicit theme; Stravinsky, however, goes much further than Adam in denaturing the ballet. Stravinsky's ballets posit things, but things stripped of their thingliness, their context of human use, and degraded to abstract forms. "I Love You" exists still, but without an "I," or a "You," or "Love." If one were to imagine a strip-tease in which a woman took off her arms and legs and replaced them with decorous plastic, Stravinsky's music would make a good accompaniment.

IV.

The Nightingale: How the Music Box Killed the Nightingale

Stravinsky's playing at the unsettled border between the natural and the unnatural can be seen most clearly in his short opera *The Nightingale*. The first act was written in 1909, before *The Firebird*; acts two and three were written in 1913-14, after *The Rite of Spring*. Here the automaton that briefly, uneasily came to life in *Petrushka*, that dwelt in *The Rite of Spring* only metaphorically, through the piston-chuggings and traffic-thunders of the music, has stepped forth and declared war on a live creature. The machine seems to be defeated; but it turns out, as we will see, that the victor and the vanquished are surprisingly difficult to tell apart.

The libretto was written by Stravinsky and his friend Mitussov, based on the famous Hans Christian Andersen fairy tale. Before Andersen's fable there was a tradition of contests between birds and artisans: for example, Crashaw's poem "Music's Duel" (1646), itself a translation of a neo-Latin poem, tells of a song-fight between a nightingale and a lutanist, in which the nightingale so exhausts itself in melody that it at last collapses, dead, upon the lute—art becomes nature's grave. But Andersen, a kind of Luddite of the imagination, contrives his story so that artifice proves unconsoling, deathly, while the real bird soothes and delights, brings the sick Emperor back to life.

Stravinsky's opera is divided between the early style of Act I and the advanced style of Acts II and III. Act I is pastoral, canorous. It begins with a tranquil Fisherman's song (used to frame the beginnings and ends of all three acts); then some courtiers appear with a cook-girl, who is to guide them to the haunts of a nightingale—rumors of the beauty of the nightingale's song have reached the court. But the courtiers are not used to the outdoors, and when they hear a frog croak they think it is a nightingale, and praise its lovely song—earlier they also made the same mistake over the mooing of a cow. The cook-girl corrects the courtiers, and eventually directs them to the nightingale. They persuade the reluctant nightingale to return with them to the court.

In Act II, we see a great pageant for the entrance of the Emperor of China—so unnatural is the court that little bells are tied to every flower. Some of the courtiers are disappointed that the nightingale is a small gray bird, nothing magnificent or shining or diamondlike. The nightingale sings an audition-aria; the Emperor weeps at the beauty, and offers the bird a reward. But the Japanese ambassadors come, bearing the gift of a mechanical nightingale; they wind it up and it sings a toy tune and it captures everyone's fancy. The real nightingale flies away unobserved, and the Emperor grants the automaton a privileged position on his nightstand.

The somber third act takes place many years later, in the Emperor's bedroom. Spectres taunt him with memories of the past; Death sits by his bedside. The real nightingale flies in the window and starts to sing; Death so enjoys the song that she offers to let the Emperor live if the nightingale will continue the music. Death disappears, after a while, and the Emperor falls asleep; the courtiers, in the midst of a funeral march, mourn the Emperor whom they think dead, but he appears before them in full regalia, bathed in light.

This plot line is a substitution-comedy, like Delibes' *Coppélia*: Stravinsky swiftly switches from the real to the artificial and back again. Clearly the effect of the opera depends on the contrast between nature and the world of the court:

> As there is no action until the second act, I told myself that it would not be unreasonable if the music of the Prologue [that is, Act I] bore a somewhat different character from that of the rest. And, indeed, the forest, with its nightingale, the pure soul of the child who falls in love with its song . . . all this gentle poetry of Hans Andersen's could not be expressed in the same way as the baroque luxury of the Chinese Court, with its bizarre etiquette, its palace fetes, its thousands of little bells and lanterns, and the grotesque humming of the mechanical Japanese nightingale . . . in short, all this exotic fantasy obviously demanded a different musical idiom. (*A* 51)

Actually, Stravinsky thought of making the bizarrerie of the court even more extravagant than it is in the finished opera. Benois, the stage designer, applauded (with some reservations) Stravinsky's idea of having the Emperor carried in on a palanquin, then inserted like a doll into his throne (*PD* 116). And Stravinsky wanted the Act II prelude to be accompanied by "Chinese shadows . . . like a magic lantern" (*PD* 118). If the opera had gone further in this direction, the Chinese court would have been reduced to a puppet-show or mere slide projection. Even as it is, when the Japanese ambassadors present the artificial nightingale to the court, they are only bringing a machine to another machine.

How does the music of the real nightingale differ from that of the mechanical? The old-fashioned means of differentiation might have been to assign diatonic music (that is, music based on the notes represented by the white keys of a piano) to the real bird, and chromatic music (all the piano-keys, black and white) to the unnatural being. Stravinsky, however, did just the opposite: the real nightingale sings swaying chromatic runs ending in swoons and droops. And the automaton (represented mostly by an oboe, but with a few cheeps from piccolo and celesta) sings crisp, clear seconds and thirds, symmetrical figures rapidly stitched up and down the staff.

The real nightingale is expressive in exactly the way that Stravinsky deprecates elsewhere—melancholy mood-music, humid music that all too slavishly illustrates the text, which tells of wet gardens shivering in the tears of a moonlit night. The mechanical nightingale sings thing-music, clean and objective, like the "Tour de Passe-passe" in *Petrushka*. And when the mechanical nightingale's song is over, the orchestra continues and intensifies the sense of mechanism: the Emperor and his retinue leave the court, accompanied by the most powerful music in the score, a *largo maestoso* march at once machine-driven and barbarous; a music-box fit for Genghis Khan. The real nightingale's music is at once flashy and slighty sodden, colorful in a bleary, Rimsky-Korsakov sort of way; while the mechanical nightingale's music sounds like the dry, learned Stravinsky of the years to come. *The Nightingale* erects a theatre of automata in order to show how smeared and faded the old operatic expressivity of the bird sounds by contrast.

It is not certain that, in 1913, Stravinsky thought of his opera as a parable about the objectivity of music; but that is what his subsequent development

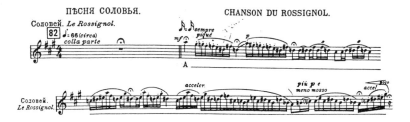

has made it become. In later life Stravinsky said of Mozart's *Die Zauber-flöte* (*The Magic Flute*, 1791) that

> . . . the intentional meaning of the opera, the triumph of Life over Death, is reversed at times in the depths of the music; in the brave little parade of Music through the gates of Death, for example, the flute charms the Keeper into a stay of execution, but the piece is a funeral march, nonetheless. (*TC* 148)

I think this is just what has happened in *The Nightingale*: the triumph of Nature over Art, described in the libretto, is reversed in the depths of the music. (In fact, the exchange of ''brave little parade'' and ''funeral march'' takes place exactly as Stravinsky describes in *Die Zauberflöte*.) The Emperor and his Court were all dead to begin with, and Life never seemed anything but an irrelevant intrusion; and Nature is the thick domain where nightingales and cows and frogs all sound approximately alike.

And yet, from another point of view, the real nightingale is not much different from the mechanical. The real bird represents subjectivity, expressiveness, but a cool, detached subjectivity, a subjectivity in the absence of a subject. The bird sings of human passion but itself feels no pang; its song is a critique or epitome of musical expression, rather than expression *per se*. If a society of dolls listened to erudite explanations of human melancholy, those dolls might imagine that the song of the real nightingale expressed sadness; but if that aria were transposed to, say, a Verdi opera, it would sound like the most frigid coloratura exercise, little different from the toy tootling of the artificial bird. The mechanical nightingale has only the briefest role in *The Nightingale*, and yet it is the opera's true hero: the action is seen from its point of view. The insertable Emperor, the pink-and-black magic-lantern décor, the Act II Prelude that sounded to Stravinsky like the ringing of a telephone (*ED* 30), all suggest a machine's fantasy of human life.

In a letter written when he sent the opera to the printer, Stravinsky remarked, ''I composed *The Nightingale* in the period of my infatuation with birds (at any rate, when I was at my bird-best)'' (*Selected Correspondence* II 199); but Stravinsky was never other than at his bird-best. Birds were a lifelong obsession, from his first success, *The Firebird*, to his last original work, *The Owl and the Pussy-Cat* (1966). The song of a bird takes place at the juncture of nature and art, and therefore is the ideal medium to test their relation.

Can a bird's song be considered music? In *Poetics of Music*, Stravinsky (or Roland-Manuel, following a suggestion of Stravinsky's) said No:

> I shall take the most banal example: that of the pleasure we experience on hearing the murmur of the breeze in the trees, the rippling of a brook, the song of a bird. All this pleases us, diverts us, delights us. We may even say: "What lovely music!" . . . These natural sounds suggest music to us, but are not yet themselves music. . . . They are promises of music; it takes a human being to keep them. (*PM* 23)

Very rarely did Stravinsky write a direct imitation of a bird's song: for example in the soprano cuckoo-calls in "When Dasies Pied"—that "word of feare,/ Unpleasing to a married eare" in the third of the *Three Songs from William Shakespeare* (1953). The cuckoo sings in falling minor thirds, just as in real life, or, at least, as in Beethoven and Berlioz. (It may be significant that here Stravinsky recalled a bird-song that inspires dread, not an exclamation of "What lovely music!") But generally Stravinsky deplored composers like Messiaen whose music was closely based on bird-songs or other sounds of nature, as he explained in an interview:

> C[ommentary Magazine].: Do you agree with Messiaen that "Nature" (he writes it in upper-case)—its sounds, colours, forms, rhythms—is the composer's supreme resource?
> I.S.: . . . I do not deny the legitimacy of Messiaen's imitations, of course, or the fertility, to him, of "natural" resources. What I do say is that no matter how faithful, these imitations are necessarily expressed in, cannot escape being contained by, the harmony, rhythm, instrumental colour, and (especially in Messiaen's case) volume of the contemporary musical language.
> C.: Do you think of "art" and "nature" as two realities, Mr. Stravinsky, and is there any act of transformation of the one in the other?
> I.S.: There are any number of realities . . . For me, music is reality, as I have said before, and like Baudelaire, but unlike Messiaen, "*J'aime mieux une boîte à musique qu'un rossignol.*" As for transformation, I do not admit the idea . . . Obviously the phenomenal world is refractable in music, or represented in it. The point is simply that I don't understand the mirroring (or the transforming) chemistry. (*D* 69-70)

"I prefer a music-box to a nightingale"—*there* is the subversive motto of Stravinsky's first opera, everywhere contradicting the moral of Andersen's fairy-tale. Stravinsky's "real" nightingale and his artificial nightingale alike are music-boxes, equally remote in tenor from the liquid siftings of actual nightingales audible in forests. (The bird is not native to America, but music lovers know its song from the field recording used in Respighi's *The*

Pines of Rome [1916].) The subject of *The Nightingale* seems to be the transformation of nature into art; but in fact the "natural" Act I is as artificial as the "artificial" Acts II and III. There is transformation, but not from nature to art, only from one system of artifice to another. Nowhere does a whiff of fresh air intrude into the music. The opera is a further demonstration of the fact that in music, no natural system can exist, no means of embracing or imitating nature can exist.

Long after *The Nightingale*, the relation of bird to machine exercised power in Stravinsky's imagination. In the 1910s Ravel was one of Stravinsky's closest friends, and it cannot have been by chance that Ravel outfitted a room of his house, in which he wanted Stravinsky to stay, with a mechanical nightingale (*C* 66). When Stravinsky moved to Hollywood, California, he noted with horror that among the appurtenances of the mortuary parlors were "Japanese electronic canaries" (*TC* 117)—perhaps a modern producer of *The Nightingale* could move the setting to Forest Lawn cemetery with little detriment to the opera's theme. Near the end of Stravinsky's life he received as a Christmas present a canary "whose finest *fioriture* seem to be mating responses to our electric juice-squeezer" (*TC* 131). The real canary's wooing of the machine is a fine pendant to the action of Stravinsky's opera: not only does Stravinsky prefer the music-box to the nightingale, but, so to speak, the nightingale itself prefers the music-box. We know that Stravinsky's favorite pet bird was a parrot—but a silent parrot, as if music constituted itself in nature's absence of sound.

In Yeats's "Sailing to Byzantium" (1927), the poet envies the state of a bird made out of gold:

> *Once out of nature I shall never take*
> *My bodily form from any natural thing,*
> *But such a form as Grecian goldsmiths make*
> *Of hammered gold and gold enamelling*
> *To keep a drowsy Emperor awake;*
> *Or set upon a golden bough to sing*
> *To lords and ladies of Byzantium*
> *Of what is past, or passing, or to come.*
>
> (Variorum Edition, *p. 408*)

Yeats, like Stravinsky, was attracted to Andersen's fairy-tale; and like Stravinsky he revised it into an ambiguous parable of the superiority of art to nature. It is possible that Stravinsky on some level felt the same wish: to *be* a mechanical bird, to identify himself with the metronome and be rid of the inaccuracies of flesh.

V.
The Wedding: The Erotics of Machines

"I prefer a music-box to a nightingale" also came to mean "I prefer a player-piano to a piano-player." From 1914 on, Stravinsky became fascinated with the pianola—indeed, when he was old, he marveled at the amount of time he had spent transcribing his works for piano-rolls. The pianola seemed to offer many advantages over other means by which music could attain acoustic realization: 1) it eliminated human interpretation, so that no middle-man interfered with the composer's plan (*A* 101); 2) it offered technical resources beyond a human pianist's wildest dreams—Stravinsky told the poet Mayakovsky that he intended to compose twenty-two hand piano music (*PD* 213); 3) its incapacity for nuances of tempo seemed right for the hard, objective music that he wanted to write (*ED* 70); 4) it seemed to be the instrument most characteristic of the modern age—"Bach wrote for the clavier because it was the instrument of his time. . . . Why, then, should I not write for the mechanical piano?" (*PD* 622). In 1922 Stravinsky decided to keep his studio in the factory where the Pleyel company made pianolas (*PD* 213)—in this fashion he managed to live inside a music-box, where he devised piano-roll perforations to his heart's delight.

Though he wrote an *Etude for Pianola* and many pianola transcriptions, the great result of his study was *The Wedding* (*Les Noces*, 1914-23). This astonishing piece, an assault of nonsense syllables, snatches of conversation, fragments of ritual, is an enactment, or cubist reconstruction, of a Russian peasant wedding, but, despite the Christian saints whose names are invoked, it might be neolithic, or Australopithecine, so backward-looking is its range of auditory allusion. We watch as the tresses of the bride are bound, and the hair of the groom slicked down with oil; the bride and groom are led to each other; the nuptial bed is warmed by a man and a woman chosen from the guests. All the action is accompanied by chatter, out of which emerges a whoop or intelligible phrase: we hear pet names, silly games (the guests prattle about strawberries that bow and talk sweetly to each other, and then remind themselves that these berries are only figures of speech for the bride and groom), much calling upon saints, much doting on the wine and the "nine kinds of beer," some veiled sexual talk. But the speeches suggest cultural complexities, not psychological ones, and the guests seem as overt and predictable as animals or dolls. The singers are not to be thought of as *dramatis personae*:

> As a collection of clichés and quotations of typical wedding sayings it [*The Wedding*] might be compared to one of those scenes in *Ulysses* in which the reader seems to be overhearing scraps of conversation without the connecting thread of discourse. . . . Individual roles do not exist in *Les Noces*, but only solo voices that impersonate now one type of character and now another. . . . the fiancé's words are sung by a tenor in the grooming scene, but by a bass at the end . . . Even the proper names in the text such as Palagai or Saveliushka belong to no one in particular. They were chosen for their sound, their syllables, and their Russian typicality. (*ED* 115)

It is a Derridian opera—the auditory equivalent of the strips of newsprint that Picasso glued to some of his canvases. The speeches lack even the faintest authority of a speaker and continually degenerate into rhythmic babble; the names of the "characters" are anonyms. Richard Taruskin has noted (in his splendid article "Stravinsky's 'Rejoicing Discovery' and What it Meant: In Defense of his Notorious Text Setting") that, in the first of the *Three Japanese Lyrics* (1913), "the verbal and musical stresses . . . cancel one another out, leaving a dynamically uninflected, stressless line, the musical equivalent of the flat surface . . . of Japanese paintings and prints" (*Stravinsky Retrospectives*, ed. Haimo and Johnson, p. 172). In *The Wedding*, the pictorial effect is different: the musical stresses do not efface the verbal ones, but squash them together into a giant word-balloon, a collage in which the texts of the under-strips are barely visible through the translucent over-strips.

Stravinsky liked the "non-personal" conception of the première: ". . . the choreography was expressed in blocks and masses; individual personalities did not, could not, emerge. . . . [It was] a stylization not unlike Kabuki theatre" (*ED* 117). I would think it was a stylization quite unlike Kabuki theatre. Stravinsky's actors were not determinate, single-thrusting, like the Japanese actors who bear their fixed identities incised on their masks or make-up; they were instead molecules unconsciously agglomerating into forceful motion. If *The Wedding* is Kabuki-like, it is Kabuki smashed into a thousand pieces that gradually reassemble before our eyes: the action is irresistible, though the actors are negligible; underneath the shouts, the exclamations, the isolated speeches a firm rhythm establishes itself and sweeps all else away.

The orchestra at the première of *The Wedding* consisted of four pianos and a battery of percussion—that is, an all-percussion orchestra, since Stravinsky regarded the piano as entirely percussive in character (*PD* 122). The orchestration of the piece vexed the composer: as early as 1917, Stravinsky had written a nearly complete score with a somewhat more traditional instrumentation; and by 1919 he had written a version of the first two of the four tableaux in which there was a prominent part for a pianola. Stravinsky abandoned this version because it was too difficult to synchronize the mechanical piano with the live instrumentalists; but anyone who has heard Robert Craft's fascinating recording (in 1974) of the 1919 score—made tangy by a cimbalom's plink and a harmonium's drone, as well as by a pianola—might think that it is potentially the most impressive of the three versions of the score.

As in *The Rite of Spring*, we see that, in Stravinsky's imagination, sexuality is intimate with the machine; the peak of the organic and the peak of the inorganic are one and the same. In Fellini's *Casanova*—a film that owes a good deal to Hoffmann's "Der Sandmann"—the hero likes to pace his sexual thrusts to the beat of a wind-up mechanical bird; and a similar sense of sexual biophysics seems to be part of Stravinsky's nature. *The Wedding* ends at the verge of a remarkable, completely unstageable spectacle: a wedding night in which mannequins copulate to the pounding of a player-piano. In the same year as the pianola version of *The Wedding*, Stravinsky considered a commission to write music for a puppet-play based on the Homeric "Battle of the Frogs and Mice" (*PD* 186); and it is certain that the idea of a fully denatured theatre was much on his mind. Some years after, when he began his career as a concert performer, he had a hallucination in the midst of playing his piano concerto: "I was suddenly obsessed by the idea that the audience was a collection of dolls in a huge panopticon" (*ED* 47). That is the logical endpoint of Stravinsky's fantasy: a theatre of faceless and nameless puppets, impelled by the rhythm of mechanical instruments, in front of an audience of dolls.

VI.

Oedipus Rex: How the Phoneme Killed the Sememe

The Wedding was among the first of many vocal works by Stravinsky that do violence to language—not only did Stravinsky wish to destroy the expressive character of sounds, he also wished to destroy the semantic character of words. Often in *The Wedding* the human voice is itself used as a percussive instrument, chugging out *ahs* and *oos* in fast thick pants. The basic unit of Stravinskian vocal music is the not the word, but the syllable—or, even less than the syllable, the phoneme (*ED* 121). The composer did what he could to frustrate the ear's desire to bind these bits of sound into meaningful propositions.

Some of the vocabulary of Stravinsky's texts consists of non-words—that is an easy way to empty language of significance. The text of *The Wedding*, and of several other works of this period, came from two anthologies of Russian folk verse. Stravinsky preferred the most nonsensical poems. In *The Wedding*, there is a word, *lushenki*, that "is a rhyming word, in fact, the diminutive of a rhyming word; it has no 'sense' " (*ED* 116). In a short suite of Russian songs called *Pribaútki* (1914)—the title refers to a verse form similar to a limerick—there appears a counting-game song, like the English "eeny, meeny, mynee, mo" (*ED* 121). Clearly Stravinsky wanted words for color, for quantitative value, for impulse, for alogical pattern. Taruskin has said of the third of the Pribaútki: "It is not about a colonel, not about a quail. It is about the letter p and . . . rhythmic groups that all end in the vowel a" (*SR* 185). No composer ever demanded language to be more docile, no composer was ever more suspicious of any insubordination of meaning in the texts he employed.

But what is disquieting about Stravinsky's vocal compositions is not that he set nonsense-texts but that he seemed to regard all texts (once incorporated into a musical composition) as nonsense. It is as if sense and music were profoundly incompatible. Music is eerily indifferent to the meaning of the texts it uses: "the words even of the Ninth Symphony [of Beethoven] can be reduced to nonsense without affecting the music" (*TC* 290).

According to Stravinsky, every composer approaches a poem intending to tear it to pieces, to purge it of meaning—or at least not minding if that is the result. The text of *The Wedding* had the great advantage that it was flayed to ribbons even before it was set to music; but Stravinsky never hesitated to perform radical surgery even on far more august words. Speaking of the final bars in the second and third movements of his *Symphony of Psalms* (1930), Stravinsky said: "I really do tire of people pointing out that *Dominum* is one word and that the meaning is obscured the way I respirate it" (*D* 46). But if a composer spreads

Do [breath]   Mi   Num

over great distances, he can expect people to wonder why the name of the Lord has been disarticulated into solmization syllables. Perhaps Stravinsky felt that he could improve the sanctity of his music to the extent that he could drain the words of their holiness.

When, after *The Wedding* and the comic operatic scene *Mavra* (1922), Stravinsky decided that Russian was no longer an acceptable medium for an international composer, he set in search of a new language. The most attractive languages, he discovered, were those that no one spoke:

> [In Genoa] I happened to find in a bookseller's a volume by Joergensen on St. Francis of Assisi . . . the familiar speech of the saint was Provençal, but . . . on solemn occasions, such as prayer, he used French. I have always considered that a special language, and not that of current converse, was required for subjects touching on the sublime. (*A* 125)

This was the origin of Stravinsky's decision to write his opera-oratorio *Oedipus Rex* (1927) to a text in Latin. He set about obtaining this text by asking Jean Cocteau, who was eager to collaborate, to write a brief version, in French, of Sophocles' Greek tragedy, and then by finding a Latinist (Jean Daniélou) to translate Cocteau's French into Latin. Certain modern poets liked to create texts thick with overtones by piling one translation on top of another: Ezra Pound, for instance, wrote *Canto* I by translating into English a passage from a Renaissance Latin translation of Homer's *Odyssey*, in order to impart a special depth to language. But the text of Stravinsky's *Oedipus Rex* uses similar means to exactly the opposite goal: each stage of its development is an evacuating, a thinning of meaning, a loss of authorial responsibility. The text attains such corruption that it becomes sublime. Stravinsky confessed that he did not know what certain passages meant, and disliked some passages that he did understand:

> [One] line mentions a "witness to the murder, who steps out from the shadows," and I have always wondered who that interesting character might be. . . . But the final "*on t'aimait* [we loved you]" is the most offensive phrase of all, for it is a journalist's caption and a blot of sentimentality . . . [concerning the phrase *omniscius pastor*, all-knowing shepherd:] *Why* the shepherd should be omniscient I do not know. (*D* 30-31)

We have, then, a version of the Oedipus story told by an ignorant, snooty, and sentimental narrator, where the musical accompaniment is (by Stravinsky's admission) a "*Merzbild*" (*D* 27) of *Folies Bergères* tunes, Wagnerian seventh-chords, florid Handelian arias, and dramatic intensification-devices out of Verdi. (The Dada collagist Kurt Schwitters liked to attach the nonsense syllable *Merz* in front of words—so a *Merzbild* is a nonsense-image.) As for the actors, Stravinsky considered many means for degrading them, too. He thought first of a performance entirely by puppets, à la Gordon Craig, or of an Oedipus masked like an Oriental sun-god (*D* 24)—as if *Oedipus Rex* were a divertissement performed for the enjoyment of the Japanese ambassadors in *The Nightingale*. Then he thought of having the singers holding up scrolls as they sang their parts (*D* 23), as if we were witnessing not a performance but a rehearsal of a performance from the fifth century B.C. Then he thought of having each actor stand behind his own private curtain, out of which he stepped before singing (*D* 23)—thereby fracturing the stage into an ensemble of tiny stages, each inhabited by its own soliloquist. At last, for the première, Cocteau designed for Oedipus a mask with pop-out eyes (*PD* 418)—the Mr. Potato Head approach to Greek tragedy. The general result of these changes is to murder Sophocles' play—to disable the action and petrify the actors, to present a dead spectacle in a dead tongue. Stravinsky aspired to make of *Oedipus Rex* a "waxworks" (*D* 24).

Why? Stravinsky was not frivolous by temperament, and had no desire to write a burlesque. If he demeaned the dignity of the actors, the narrator, and even the musicians, it was because he wanted to represent on stage something from which the actors, the narrator, the musicians might distract:

> I consider this static representation a more vital way to focus the tragedy not on Oedipus himself and the other individuals, but on the "fatal development"

that, for me, is the meaning of the play. . . . My audience is not indifferent to the fate of the person, but I think it far more concerned with the person of the fate . . . the stage figures are more dramatically isolated and helpless precisely because they are plastically mute . . . Crossroads are not personal but geometrical, and the geometry of tragedy, the inevitable intersecting of lines, is what concerned me. (*D* 24)

Just as, in *The Rite of Spring*, the individuals were effaced so that the energy within them might leap forth, so in *Oedipus Rex* the dramatis personae are made to shrink into a musico-mathematical notation of fate's vectors. We see not "Oedipus" but a showy tenor who keeps singing *Ego clarissimus Oedipus* ("I, most illustrious Oedipus"), overinsisting on the character's name but not persuading us that he has assumed the character's identity. We hear the *fioriture* that, in a Handel opera, would be expressive of pride; but here they sound like a bad singer's rote performance of Handel. Temporarily Fate takes the role of Creon, or Oedipus, or Jocasta—or, as Shepherd and Messenger, sings a duet with itself; but there are no individuals, there is only a grand objectivity that briefly falls into an illusion of various subjects. *Oedipus Rex* is a kind of machine that erects characters, pushes them forth, and at last annihilates them—an iron maiden, a rack for the dismemberment of puppets.

Cocteau's stingy, skeletal, "unmusical" (by Cocteau's own admission) text greatly assisted Stravinsky's assault against dramatic character. A normal dramatist, adapting Greek tragedy to a puppet-stage, would take out the verbal flourishes and strip the play to bare action; Cocteau, however, emptied the play of action and left only a few withered flowers of rhetoric. The commonest word in the text is *dicere*—everyone *says*, or *answers*, or *reports*, or *speaks*, or *refuses to speak*, or *tells true*, or *tells false*, no one *does*. Only one character is actually named the Messenger; but in fact everyone except Oedipus is a message-conveyor or a message-frustrator. Creon's aria begins *Respondit deus* ("the god answers"), as he reports the oracle's message—the plague will only end when Laius' murderer is found; the chorus then mutters *Deus dixit, dixit, dixit* ("the god said, said, said"). Then Tiresias enters; his aria begins *Dicere non possum* ("I cannot say"), and he refuses to speak until Oedipus accuses him of the murder of Laius—at last Oedipus' taunt forces him to utter (*Dicam*, "I shall speak") the terrible truth, that the king's murderer is himself a king. This rhythm of speech-giving and speech-withholding continues through the opera—in Act II Jocasta tries to block messages, to discredit them, while the Messenger and the Shepherd try to utter what they know.

László Somfai, in his seminal article "Sprache, Wort und Phonem im vokalen Spätwerk Strawinskys" (from R. Stephan, ed., *Über Musik und*

Sprache, p. 34), has called attention to Stravinsky's habit of setting to music the peripheral elements of texts—such as (in *Threni*, 1958) titles and chapter-numbers—as part of a strategy of depersonifying music. Somfai also points to Stravinsky's calculated reversal of the audience's expectation (in the second part of *A Sermon, a Narrative, and a Prayer*, 1962) when the tenor, who "plays" the role of the martyr Stephen, at last sings the phrase *he fell asleep*—as if Stephen suddenly became the narrator of his own death. *Oedipus Rex* is, similarly, a depersonified opera, an opera of speeches in quotation marks. The only words that signify are the gods' words; the characters in the opera are only playback devices (or erasing devices) for speeches that are not their own. Somfai notes that in *Abraham and Isaac* (1964)—a setting of the original Hebrew text—the most salient musical phrase accompanies the much-repeated word *Vayomer* ("he said"); and the continual emphasis in *Oedipus Rex* on *dic, dixit, dicere, dico* and so forth anticipates this device. The fact of speaking seems of greater interest to Stravinsky than the content of what is spoken. Speech does not belong to anyone in particular, but inhabits a huge, anonymous space.

Stravinsky's chief device for anonymizing the text consists of bizarrely varied repetition. For example, the chorus will hear a word from an aria—itself only a quotation—and requote it over and over again, draining it of whatever relation it once had to a particular speaker. Often these repetitions, whether choral or solo, will keep changing in meter: an obvious instance occurs when the chorus hears Jocasta sing of the crossroads (*trivium*) where Laius was murdered, and hollowly repeats *trivium*, first as a dactyl, then as an anapest. One perceptive critic, Mathias Hansen (in " '. . . Stille anonyme Formeln einer entlegenen Zeit . . .': Analytische Bemerkungen zu Vertonungsprinzipien Igor Strawinskys im 'Ödipus Rex' ") has made a catalogue of the compulsive re-accentuations of key phrases in the opera. Hansen seems partly to accept Somfai's belief that by this meter-play Stravinsky intended to intensify the meaning of these words, but he also argues that "through the alteration of stress there comes about, proceeding from the alteration of the musical accenting, an alienation [*Verfremdung*] of the verbal message" (*Arbeitsheft 35, Musikalische Analyse in der Diskussion*, ed. Mathias Hansen, p. 61). Hansen remarks earlier in his essay, discussing Creon's aria, that the articulation of the musical form has no relation to the divisions of the text, and that this incongruity is one of Stravinsky's techniques for achieving an effect of distancing (*MAD* 54).

This seems to me the correct road to interpretation; and one might go down it still further. Hansen's model for Stravinsky's dramatic art seems to be the practice of Brecht: the audience is not encouraged to identify itself with the characters, but to contemplate the message objectively; indeed

Hansen applauds Stravinsky for creating an "effective corrective" to the "misuse of myth and history as an apology or at least a veiling of bourgeois reality . . . a religious-regressive defense of master-and-servant relations" (*MAD* 62). I see *Oedipus Rex* as a work engaged in a far broader attack, an attack on language itself. A modern audience, hearing the word *trivium* over and over again, may meditate on the significance of "crossroads"; or it may think of the most available homophone in all European languages, *trivial*. I think this textual debasement was part of Stravinsky's intention.

Stravinsky was not a Latinist, but as a well-educated man he knew that Latin poetry is strictly governed by the quantity of syllables: long syllables must be pronounced twice as long as short syllables. The queasy shiftings of syllabic patterns from one repetition to the next seem to imply that neither the chorus nor the actors quite know the language that they speak: they keep searching for a meter but not finding it, for the meter lies beneath them, in the music, unavailable to speech. The incongruity between language and music is no mere device for estranging an audience, for hindering empathy; it suggests how little relation is possible between the basic structure of music and that of language. The inner drama lies in the pounding pulse of the music, and the speakers try as best they can to accommodate their ugly, deliberately inept language to it. Sometimes (as in *Delie, exspectamus*) the chorus seems partly to succeed at aligning itself with fate's underpulse; but even in that powerful utterance the speech is squeezed onto a musical grid in 9/8 and 6/8 meter, radically asymmetrical with respect to any metrical scheme from classical tragedy (I give the prosodic duration above the line, the musical duration below):

Dē-lĭ-ĕ,   ēx-spēc-tā-mŭs,   Mĭ-nē-rvă fĭ-lĭ-ă Iŏ-vĭs, Dĭ-ān-ă

At the beginning, the chorus sings oddly punctuated phrases, of three, four, eight, or nine syllables, strung out irregularly over the orchestra's steady tribrachs. Taruskin has noted Stravinsky's tendency, in many compositions, to assign a single note-value to each syllable: "every syllable [in one of the *Pribaútki*] carries the same duration—an eighth note" (*SR* 186). In these lines, prosody is similarly flattened, except for the occasional quarter-note (*Mi*nerva filia *Io*vis, *Di*ana), seemingly thrown in as an allusion to classical scansion but without regard to the actual quantity of the sung syllable. (Cocteau's Latinized text is, of course, simply chopped prose, with no quantitative regularity.)

This chorus is a serious parody of a Greek chorus. But most of the arias illustrate a more violent struggle against the musical meter. Oedipus himself, the main actor in the play, never reaches even the slightest accommo-

dation with the music, until his final phrase. When he shouts, when he curses, when he preens himself as a coloratura tenor—when he insists on his private *melos*—he is impeding the drama. At one point he even steps out of the music entirely, and declaims, to no particular pitch, *Stipendarius es, Tiresia!* ("You are a mercenary, Tiresias!")—as if he disdained to take further part in the opera. But when, in his last words, he resigns himself to the subsistent rhythm, he advances the drama. There are many moments in the opera when truth—which is here a property only of music, never of words—is represented by some extremely simple, insistent musical device: for example, when the Shepherd and the Messenger deliver the horrifying message that Oedipus was not the son of Polybus, an emphatic C-major scale descends in the bass. And when Oedipus understands everything, his self-abandonment is represented by his resignation to a plain B-minor triad, *Lux facta est*—"light breaks." The words of Cocteau's text exist only to illustrate the collapse of rhetoric, the priority of music over speech.

There are other impediments to audience comprehension besides the choice of language and the continual misaccenting. Much of the text is obscured by the peculiarities of the vocal line—without the narrator, feeble and foolish as he is, even an audience of Latin scholars might have difficulty

in following the "action." In Jocasta's great aria, for instance, she keeps intoning, at the very lowest register of her voice,

o   ra   cu   la   o   ra   cu   la   o   ra   cu   la

with such evenness of pulse that the line might as well be

la   la   la   la   la   la   la   la   la   la   la   la

She is far too oracular to be understood. The burden of her message is, "Oracles are liars," but in the general mess of the text the oracle seems no more true or false than any other proposition. As is usual in Stravinsky's mature vocal music, the words are in danger of separating into a heap of syllables:

> Much to the contrary of the traditional concept, which submits music to the psychological expressiveness or to the dramatic significance of the word, in my *Oedipus Rex* the word is pure material, functioning musically like a block of marble or stone in a work of sculpture or architecture. (*PD* 205)

> What a joy it is to compose music to a language of convention, almost of ritual, the very nature of which imposes a lofty dignity! One no longer feels dominated by the phrase, the literal meaning . . . The text thus becomes purely phonetic material for the composer. (*A* 128)

Just as the actors are reduced to puppets, or human surrogates for puppets, so the words are demoted to things: bits of marble or stone, ground up into the concrete from which the music is built.

The advantage of a corpse-language is that it does not resist further decomposition. Modern languages have sinew, tensile strength; but Latin has such advanced rigor mortis that it could shatter into syllables without much effort. Stravinsky found that Latin was even better than nonsense, in that its decline into meaninglessness, pure sonority, was exciting. To kill words was more exhilarating than to find dead syllables. Stravinsky thought of vocal composition as a struggle for dominance between the composer and the librettist, as we can see in a note he gave to Roland-Manuel to help with the writing of *Poetics of Music*:

> The musician can approach the words that he puts to music in two ways. First, the word can be treated as sonorous material of expression itself. . . . Second, the word can determine the meaning of the music, [in which case] it is left meaningless without the word. The second approach is the passive one. The active approach is that of the musician who employs the word as sonorous material *only*, taking no account of its literal significance. (*SC* II 508)

Oedipus Rex shows signs of a fight for authority between Sophocles and Stravinsky, in which Sophocles' words are mangled by condensation, mistranslation, contorted musical setting, so the drama behind the words, the drama obscured by the words, might be elucidated.

Obviously, however, Stravinsky could not spend the rest of his career setting texts in bastardized Latin. Over the course of his career, he wrote pieces in French, English, Russian, Latin, Slavonic (in *Ave Maria* [1934]), Hebrew (in *Abraham and Isaac*), Italian (in his reworking of the Pergolesi songs in *Pulcinella* [1919]), and even German—not long before his death, he orchestrated two songs by Hugo Wolf (1968)—as if, by continually changing languages, he need not commit himself to any language in particular. But of all these languages, the abrupt, blustery, crabbed, curious Latin of *Oedipus Rex* seemed the most suitable to his strange requirements—nowhere else is his vocal music quite so daring, so sure of its asemantic, instrumentalized character.

But there are hints that he craved a language even more objective, even narrower in its width of denotation, than the pop-Latin of Cocteau and Daniélou:

> N[ew].Y[ork].R[eview].: What did you mean . . . when you declared your disbelief in words? Is it a question of their inexactness?
> I.S.: They are not so much inexact as metaphorical; not so much another form

of notation as an irrelevant and unedifying form. Sometimes I feel like those old men Gulliver encounters in the *Voyage to Laputa*, who have renounced language and who try to converse by means of objects themselves. A composer is always in that position: he has no verbal control over his music. (*D* 62)

Here Stravinsky complained of the inadequacy of words to comment on music; but there is evidence that he also would have liked to have available for use in musical composition some language akin to the bag of objects that the philosophers of Swift's Academy of Lagado haul on their backs—a thing-language. In 1953 Boston University proposed to commission Stravinsky and Dylan Thomas to write an opera, and both parties were eager:

"His" opera was to be about the rediscovery of our planet following an atomic misadventure. There would be a re-creation of language, only the new one would have no abstractions; there would be only people, objects, and words. He promised to avoid poetic indulgences: "No conceits, I'll knock them all on the head." (*C* 78)

Thomas died before they could begin; but this opera about the destruction and re-invention of language would have made explicit a theme latent in many of Stravinsky's works. This pared-down tongue, incapable of any speech-act except the starkest reference, would have been a metaphor for the general demotion of words to sound-concretions.

Stravinsky began *An Autobiography* with an odd account of his earliest memory of sound:

I can see it now. An enormous peasant seated on the stump of a tree. . . . He was dumb, but he had a way of clicking his tongue very noisily . . . he would begin to sing. This song was composed of two syllables, the only ones he could pronounce. They were devoid of any meaning, but he made them alternate with incredible dexterity in a very rapid tempo. He used to accompany this clucking in the following way: pressing the palm of his right hand under his left armpit, he would work his left arm . . . he extracted a succession of sounds . . . which might be euphemistically described as resounding kisses. (*A* 3-4)

It is as if the world begins, and the world ends, to the tune of clucks and farts. *There* is the only real language; all else is literary artifice. Stravinsky once said that, as a composer, he took very literally the Bible-verse "In the beginning was the word" (*D* 22); but that aboriginal word is more like an imbecile's rude noise, or like the half-language of a ruined earth, than like a theologian's subtle formulations of the Logos.

Sometimes Stravinsky's vocal music simply sinks into a sub-language of clucks—most notably in his barnyard fable *Renard* (1915), where the Cock goes "Chuck-chuck-chuck-a-dah," and the animal musicians imitate musical instruments: "Plinc, plinc," "zoum! zoum! patazoum!" But often Stravinsky set modern-language texts of a much more highfalutin kind, as in *Perséphone* (1934); Stravinsky thought that André Gide's libretto consisted of "*vers de caramel*," but the composer did little to unsugar the melodrama. It seems that Stravinsky wished to demonstrate the sad incompetence of modern speech, its slackness and artificiality. Lacking true concreteness, lacking any firmness of reference, modern languages must be made to display their eviscerated state.

And yet, Stravinsky loved words precisely because they failed to mean anything much. Nonsense, tongue-clicks, advanced literary discourse, have this in common: they fail to mean:

> Doubtless you recall the discussion in the *Cratylus*, Socrates refereeing at first, then refuting Hermogenes' argument that names are not attached to things by nature but are conventions of the users? Well, so far as my *art* is concerned I am on the side of Hermogenes, even though he is opposed by modern philology, which holds that names possess "echoic" value and that word conventions are anything but arbitrary . . . Derivations in nature are not the artist's affair, nature being only another convention to him. (*TC* 88-89)

Word and thing are unrelated—or, to put it another way, a word is a thing essentially alien to that other thing that claims to be its referent in the world of experience. Language, therefore, is music. It is music deficient in pitch and infirm in rhythm, but music nonetheless. All the distortions in Stravinsky's vocal lines—syllabic misemphases, melismata, dissection of words—can be justified: for if language is an arbitrary system, there is no reason not to refit its acoustic matter into another arbitrary system, invented by Stravinsky for a certain composition. By exerting extraordinary stress on language, Stravinsky proved its plasticity, its detachability from the world of its reference.

In 1944, the American composer-conductor Nathaniel Schilkret (who conducted the first recording of Gershwin's *An American in Paris*) commissioned Stravinsky, Schoenberg, and five others to write a movement each for a suite based on the book of Genesis. Stravinsky wrote a brief cantata, *Babel* (1945)—his first use of an English text. I know of no other version of the story which so rejoices in the confounding of human language: the music that accompanies the building of the tower is smooth, quiet, with little profile; but the music that accompanies the destruction of speech is kinetic, propulsive—the dismemberment of speech is every bit as exciting as the dismemberment of Orpheus in Stravinsky's ballet of 1948. Later, Stravinsky wrote that he liked hearing his works performed untranslated, in the various original languages of their composition: "musically speaking, Babel is a blessing" (*C* 35). The fall of the Tower of Babel is a Fortunate Fall: for in the scattering of the tongues language lost its canonical relation to nature, became suitable for song. "Music is a non-analogous system—or several non-analogous systems: it is more of a Babel than a universal language" (*TC* 146). Therefore *Babel*, like *Apollo*, is a parable about the origin of music. It is the Old Testament account of the creation of the unnatural.

Once the inconvenient illusion of meaning has been dispelled, a word can be taken for what it really is: a suggestion of rhythm. Stravinsky dismissed semantics as an idle exercise in besmudging sounds with a pollen of signification; but he believed that prosody was a serious discipline. In Eden, Adam fastened names to things; in Babylon, God unfastened the names and gave them rhythmic force.

His concern with prosody was lifelong. In 1914, Stravinsky decided to compose music for a passage from a book of humorous and nonsensical Russian verse called *Koz'ma Prutkov*; this project never came to fruition, but some sketches survive, with examples in musical notation of trochaics, dactyls, and anapests (*PD* 133). In *Oedipus Rex*, Stravinsky said that he based his rhythms on the meters of Sophocles' Greek choruses (*D* 29)—though this refers only to the dactylic underpulse, for Stravinsky paid, as we have seen, no attention to the scansion of the Latin text he was in fact setting to music. Indeed, his habit of ignoring tonic accent sometimes came to embarrass him: for instance, by stressing the first syllable of *cecidi* in *ego senem cecidi*, Stravinsky made his phrase mean (meaninglessly) *I fell the old man*, instead of *I killed the old man* (*MC* 150). But this did not so distress the composer that he bothered to change the music.

Why should a composer obsessed with prosody disregard the actual prosodic values of the words before him? He seems to have felt that any given word makes a botch of its own rhythm, just as it makes a botch of its meaning. Beneath a verbal phrase, there is a push, a division, an inflection; but if the syllables must be finagled to make explicit this subsistent rhythm, Stravinsky did not object to finagling them. Stravinsky admired the famous phonograph record of Yeats reading his verse:

> Yeats pauses at the end of each line, he dwells a precise time on and in between each word—one could as easily notate his verses in musical rhythm as scan them in poetic metres. (*C* 120)

Stravinsky was quite correct—perhaps he did not know that, in collaboration with Florence Farr, Yeats had in fact converted some of his poems to

musical notation, to be chanted to a psaltery. But Yeats's strange, neo-quan-
titative reading style—he pretended that English syllables, like Latin, must
be either half-notes or quarter-notes—was as much a willful imposition of
scansion as any passage of *Oedipus Rex*. Prosody exists at the place where
music and poetry join together, where they display their pure arbitrariness
unimₚeded by expression, or meaning, or even particular sounds: the
daDAdaDA without da or DA.

The study of prosody informed Stravinsky's instrumental compositions
as well as his vocal. His first important work after *Oedipus Rex* was the ballet *Apollo* (1928), which begins with the birth of Apollo and offers a pageant of the Muses, displaying their arts to the new-born god:

> The real subject of *Apollo* . . . is versification, which implies something
> arbitrary and artificial to most people, though to me art is arbitrary and must
> be artificial. The basic rhythmic patterns are iambic, and the individual
> dances may be thought of as variations of the reversible dotted-rhythm iamb
> idea. . . . I cannot say whether the idea of the Alexandrines, that supremely
> arbitrary set of prosodic rules, was pre-compositional or not . . . (*D* 33)

Apollo is a sort of poem without words, a delicate string-filigree of intersecting meters, as if the pattern of macrons and breves written out above
some lines of verse were looped over a musical staff. The action of the ballet
is a rehearsal of an aesthetic equation, Calliope + Polyhymnia =
Terpsichore:

> Calliope, receiving the stylus and tablets from Apollo, personifies poetry and
> its rhythm; Polyhymnia, finger on lips, represents mime. . . . Finally, Terp-
> sichore, combining in herself both the rhythm of poetry and the eloquence of
> gesture, reveals dancing to the world . . . (*A* 134)

Oedipus Rex is loud classicism; *Apollo* is hushed classicism. The opera is
propelled by the tension between the words, which try to assert their own
meters, their own meanings, and the music, which insists far more emphatically on its own immitigable rhythms. The ballet, however, is poised,
elegant, still; nothing contradicts the iambs proposed by the unanimous
strings.

Behind *Oedipus Rex* is Sophocles. Behind *Apollo* is the seventeenth-cen-
tury French poet Boileau, one of whose couplets is used as an epigraph to
the "Variation of Calliope":

> *Que toujours dans vos vers le sens, coupant les mots,*
> *Suspende l'hémistiche, en marque le repos.*

(L'Art poétique I 105-6)

Boileau was not the greatest poet of his time, but he was the greatest legislator of poets—he sought to give order and symmetry, propriety to verse. In the quoted couplet Boileau asked poets to devise alexandrines that fall sensibly into two equal six-syllabled half-lines. Stravinsky designed the "Variation of Calliope" to be a musical exposition of this motto (*D* 33). The score of *Apollo* is a meditation on the theme of making up rules—indefensible rules, unnatural rules, arbitrary rules, but rules without which art is impossible. Apollo is born, not in a sunburst or a clang of the spheres, but quietly, a little god in the costume of Boileau or Alexander Pope, with a powdered wig.

Stravinsky's concept of mute prosody, poetry with a finger on its lips, extended beyond *Apollo*. His *Duo Concertant* for violin and piano (1934) was composed as a "musical parallel to the old pastoral poetry" (*A* 171); among its movements are two Eglogues and a Dithyrambe. And twenty years after *Apollo*, Stravinsky wrote another classical ballet, *Orpheus* (1948), in which the theme of music-by-rule alters into the theme of rule-by-music, for Orpheus' lyre can tame savage beasts, can make trees pull their roots from the ground and walk. *Orpheus*, however, is a far more anguished ballet than its predecessor: by introducing a human being into the divine vibrations of musical action, Stravinsky introduces desperation, ecstasy, madness, all that Apollo blissfully ignored. The dismemberment of Orpheus—the climax of the ballet—shows, yet again, that human subjects and their expressive clamor cannot sustain themselves in the ether of music. Just as Oedipus' words had to be disarticulated, just as Petrushka's sawdust had to be knocked out of him, so Orpheus' crazy pain must be liquidated into the calm plinks of a harp:

> Lost in his immeasurable grief, he scorns the Bacchantes, the jealous Thracian women, and in a frenzy they tear him to pieces. Orpheus is no more, but his song lives. Apollo appears radiant in sunlight, the god raises the lyre of Orpheus, lifting his deathless song to the eternal sky. (*PD* 381)

Boileau triumphs and Dionysus, the god of expression (see *A* 100), is defeated. After *Oedipus Rex*, Stravinsky's music was mostly depopulated, disengaged, inward-turned, serenely investigating the principles of its own composition. But with *Orpheus* that unkillable phantom, the human subject, returns to disturb the prosody of the music; a revenant that foreshadows the drama of the greatest project of Stravinsky's life, *The Rake's Progress*.

VII.
The Origin of *The Rake's Progress*

The Rake's Progress (1951) is the only work of Stravinsky's that provides a full evening's entertainment—it is over twice as long as any other of his compositions. Whereas most of Stravinsky's other vocal stage works are hybrids—opera-ballet (*The Wedding, The Nightingale*), or opera-oratorio (*Oedipus Rex*), or opera-melodrama (*Perséphone*)—*The Rake's Progress* is an old-fashioned eighteenth-century "numbers" opera, divided into arias, duets, and recitative. It is a conventional work. But, to Stravinsky, music *is* Convention—there is no Nature to which music can hope to appeal. The theme of *The Rake's Progress* is conventionality, for its hero is confounded by his attempts to be spontaneous, free, governed by nature rather than by rule.

In 1947 Stravinsky saw an exhibition in Chicago of the celebrated series of eight paintings by Hogarth, *A Rake's Progress* (1733), in which a young man inherits his father's estate and seduces a town-girl, learns good manners, roisters about with whores, is arrested for debt (the town-girl ransoms him with her savings), marries an ugly rich woman (the town-girl, their child in her arms, is excluded from the ceremony), loses a second fortune in a gaming house, is sent to prison for debt, and is at last committed to the madhouse, where the town-girl continues to visit him. Hogarth's rake is a pale, inert figure surrounded everywhere by grotesques, gargoyles, who at last tear him asunder—the narrative must have seemed to Stravinsky partly parallel to the theme of the ballet that he was writing, *Orpheus*. When Stravinsky asked his friend Aldous Huxley to recommend a librettist, Huxley mentioned W. H. Auden, who, on inquiry, was eager to collaborate. I wonder whether Stravinsky or Auden ever noticed that, in the fine print on a long scroll on the second of the *Rake's Progress* paintings, Hogarth listed a gift to an Italian opera singer, namely a gold snuff box decorated with an image of Orpheus.

Auden came from New York to California to work on the scenario as a guest at Stravinsky's home; the poet amazed the composer with his erudition, his technical facility in verse, his poor personal hygiene, and his odd beliefs, as in the telepathic powers of cats (*MC* 157). Soon they expanded Hogarth's slender outline into a plot—their original scenario has been printed, with some errors (*MC* 167-76). Hogarth's story has no conflict, except that provided by the contrast between the town-girl's restraint and fidelity, opposing the rake's licentiousness; but Auden and Stravinsky outfitted the tale with a whistling villain (who eventually became the jolliest, most major-mode devil in the operatic literature) to conduct the hero to his ruin.

Most of the newly devised scenes show the hero pushing at the limits of the human condition. Hogarth's rake had fairly pedestrian desires—a little excitement, a little wealth, a little whoring, a respectable marriage; but Stravinsky's and Auden's hero, Tom Rakewell, dreams of restoring mankind to paradise, by means of a machine that extracts gold from sea-water (in the finished opera, a machine that turns stones into bread). Tom Rakewell is metaphysically ambitious in a way impossible to Hogarth's rake; behind Tom is Adonis, Adam, the Everyman of the old morality play, a whole assortment of modernist archetypes, just as the flaccid characters of Eliot's *The Waste Land* are held upright by the mythological beings to whom they allude. It has often been noted that *The Rake's Progress*, like Stravinsky's *The Soldier's Tale* (1918), is a Faust tale—indeed T. S. Eliot thought that the libretto failed in its attempt to combine Hogarth's narrative with the traditional pact with the devil (*PD* 540). But it is specifically a Faust story on the model of Goethe, for Tom Rakewell, like Goethe's Faust, is a creature of unlimited desire, tottering on a confused path to the verge of ultimate things.

Stravinsky knew almost nothing about Auden before inviting him to write a libretto. He was amazingly lucky, for it happened that Auden shared many of Stravinsky's opinions about the virtues of the conventional and about the relation between nature and art. In his essay "Making, Knowing, and Judging," Auden offered a brief test to determine whether a man's assumptions about art were compatible with his own:

"Do you like, and by like I mean really like . . .
1) Long lists of proper names such as the Old Testament genealogies or the Catalogue of ships in the *Iliad*?

2) Riddles and all other ways of not calling a spade a spade?
3) Complicated verse forms of great technical difficulty . . .?
4) Conscious theatrical exaggeration, pieces of Baroque flattery . . .?'' (*The Dyer's Hand*, pp. 47-48)

To anyone who answered Yes to all four, who delighted in language's unmeaning self-delight, Auden felt sympathetic. It is a test that Stravinsky could have passed effortlessly. Auden, like Goethe, thought that Art is Art because it is not Nature, and relegated Art to its own private sphere of operation, what he called the Secondary World.

Auden's attitude toward the Primary World—Nature—was uneasy. He was an avid student of biology, psychology, and (from child's guides) physics; and he generally saw Nature as inhuman, unpleasant, difficult to apprehend, ruled by impersonal forces such as gravitation, sexual desire, and evolutionary survival-urges. Opposed to this species of Nature is Spirit:

The Two Real Worlds
1) The Natural World of the Dynamo, the world of masses, identical relations and recurrent events, describable, not in words but in terms of numbers, or rather, in algebraic terms. . . .
2) The Historical World of the Virgin, the world of faces, analogical relations and singular events, describable only in terms of speech. (*DH* 61)

In this essay, "The Virgin and the Dynamo," Auden went on to posit two chimerical worlds, one caused by the false attempt to personalize the Dynamo, to pretend that masses have faces, as if the force of gravity might be swayed by fervent prayer—the other caused by the false attempt to depersonalize the Virgin, to treat human beings as statistical abstractions, the pawns of impulse, in the manner of Zola. This dialectic of Nature and Spirit was an attempt to discover how a Christian might do justice both to his soul—unique and personal—and to his body—material and animal, subject to biophysical laws.

But Auden had an aesthetic dialectic as well as a Christian dialectic. Here we have, not Nature vs. Spirit, but Nature vs. Art. Here Nature is not so much a physicist's abstraction of vectors colliding on a three-dimensional grid, but a kind of chaos, sloppy and wet, unintelligible, weedy, a landscape without a gardener. Art, on the other hand, is exactly the opposite: spruce and spiffy, in fact a bit too neat, for the privet is always perfectly cut and the good guy always gets the girl at the end of the story.

Auden thought, correctly, that his greatest work was *The Sea and the Mirror* (1944), which is his fullest statement of the relation of Nature to Art. It is a "Commentary" on Shakespeare's *The Tempest*, in which Auden resurrects the dramatis personae and requires each one to comment, in his own voice, on the action of the play. The subtlest of the commentators is, surprisingly, Caliban, who gives a long speech in the most florid, baroque, Henry-Jamesish prose. Caliban claims that Shakespeare spoiled his play by introducing into it a personification of Nature, Caliban himself—for lumpish, unlovely Nature is the one thing that resists all of the transforming magic of Art, the brute guest at the cocktail party of the Muses. In fact Nature and Art are hopeless opposites:

> You yourself [Shakespeare], we seem to remember, have spoken of the conjured spectacle as "a mirror held up to nature," a phrase misleading in its aphoristic sweep but indicative at least of one aspect of the relation between the real and the imagined, their mutual reversal of value, for isn't the essential artistic strangeness to which your citation of the sinisterly blessed image would point just this: that on the far side of the mirror the general will to compose, to form at all costs a felicitous pattern becomes the *necessary cause* of any particular effort to live or act or love or triumph or vary, instead of being as, in so far as it emerges at all, it is on this side, their *accidental effect*? (*Collected Poems*, p. 330)

Nature is a chaos struggling toward order; Art is a backward image of Nature, for Art begins in order, in intendedness, and struggles to diversify itself into a semblance of the richness and variety of Nature.

Caliban goes on to show the horrors of strictly unnatural Art and of strictly artless Nature. If Ariel, the artistic imagination, becomes the dominant force in a man's being, that man will live in an endless dream, where fantastic images form and teem and vanish without any standard of reality or truth. But to a man in whom Caliban predominates, a man without imagination, Nature reveals itself to be a waste land of extinct volcanos, an airless lava plateau—a scientist's caricature of the physical world. Ariel's feeling for the ideal is needed to soften the asperity of Nature; and Caliban's sense of fact is needed to anchor, secure, and validate the imagination's intuitions.

These two dialectics—the Virgin and the Dynamo, and Ariel and Caliban—govern the Progress of Tom Rakewell. Though Stravinsky helped with the construction of the scenario, and Auden's friend Chester Kallman wrote much of the libretto—including some of its best scenes—there is nothing in *The Rake's Progress* that falls outside the orbit of Auden's intellectual world. Anne Trulove, the opera's heroine (Hogarth's town-girl moved into the country and made chaste) is the Virgin of Auden's dialectic, a respecter of the soul's uniqueness, a Mary-like intercessor for Tom's salvation; whereas Tom, the nature-child, embodies the values of the Dynamo. By another analysis, as we shall see, Tom is Caliban, while Nick Shadow, the Devil, is a sinister Ariel, provoking outlandish images of bliss.

Some critics (such as Gabriel Josipovici, in Paul Griffiths' *Igor Stravinsky: The Rake's Progress*, p. 73) have seen the opera, at least in part, as warm, subjective, psychological, "human and haunting," and to that extent a repudiation of the heartless objective music of Stravinsky's earlier days. I hope to show the opposite: that while the libretto, like the libretto of *The Nightingale*, seems to illustrate the victory of the human over the inhuman, the opera as a whole celebrates system and inflexible rule.

The characters of the opera are colder than they first appear. As far as Auden was concerned, there are two types of drama: objective drama (the detestable kind), in which the playwright carries a camera and tape-recorder to study human behavior at a far remove; and subjective drama (the good kind), in which the playwright illuminates the human ego exercising its freedom by making choices:

> If I try . . . to project my subjective experience of life in dramatic form the play will be of the allegorical type like Everyman. The hero will be the volitional ego that chooses, and the other characters, either states of the self, pleasant and unpleasant, good and bad, for or against which the hero's choices are made, or counselors, like reason and conscience, which attempt to influence his choices. (*DH* 172)

The Rake's Progress is clearly a "subjective" drama; but it is subjectivity objectified, picked apart, projected into a battery of allegorical figments. Pathos is diminished, in the absence of any independent agent except the hero. In Auden's view, almost every interesting story is secretly a *psychomachia*, a battle of internal forces within a single soul. Thus he described Don Quixote and Sancho Panza as the twin aspects of a single being, one a mad improver of life and the other a lax bland realist; similarly twinned are Don Giovanni and Leporello, Lear and his Fool, Tamino and Papageno (in Mozart's *Die Zauberflöte*), Bertie Wooster and Jeeves. (All these are discussed in the essay "Balaam and his Ass.")

But the most important pair of master and servant, for our purposes, is Goethe's Faust-Mephistophiles. Auden would have them played by "identical twins" (*DH* 116), for they are alike in that each is fundamentally a nonentity:

> . . . the story of Faust is precisely the story of a man who refuses to be anyone and only wishes to be someone else . . . Mephisto . . . [is] the manifestation of possibility without actuality . . . (*DH* 115)

In our age . . . Our real, because permanent, idolatry is an idolatry of possibility. And in such an age the Devil appears in the form of Mephisto, in the form, that is, of an actor. The point about an actor is that he has no name of his own, for his name is Legion. One might say that our age recognized its nature on the day when Henry Irving was knighted. (*DH* 118)

The Rake's Progress was Auden's contribution to the literature of non-persons. Neither its hero nor its villain is anything but a pregnant zero, a creature shapeless with unreal potentialities. Stravinsky had long worked toward a theatre of inexpressiveness; and at last he had a libretto crammed with histrionic opportunities, but populated only with generic, brand-x human beings, characters who secretly lack identity. *Petrushka* treated puppets; *The Nightingale* treated machines; *The Rake's Progress* treats actors, toying with roles, conniving at the crowd.

VIII.

The Rake's Progress, Act I: Pastoral and Mock Pastoral

Act I, scene 1. The opera opens in cool pastoral, at the garden of Trulove's house. Anne and Tom sing a duet about Aphrodite, who will "with a kiss restore the Age of Gold." The duet becomes a trio as the prudent Trulove worries whether Tom can keep his vows to his daughter Anne—*vow* is one of the crucial words of the opera, for behavior that is constrained, circumscribed by vows differs from the radically free behavior that Tom will cultivate; *vow* is convention, *freedom* is its opposite. Trulove has found Tom a job in a counting-house, but Tom declines—in a soliloquy-aria, Tom scoffs at steady employment:

> *Since it is not by merit*
> *We rise or we fall,*
> *But the favour of Fortune*
> *That governs us all,*
> *Why should I labour*
> *For what in the end*
> *She will give me for nothing*
> *If she be my friend? . . .*
> *My life lies before me.*
> *The world is so wide:*
> *Come, wishes, be horses;*
> *This beggar shall ride.*
> *[recit.] I wish I had money.*

Tom trusts heaven's "predestination" to determine his fate. One of Ho-

48

garth's paintings is called "The Gaming House"; and while there is no gaming-house in the opera (the official gambling scene takes place in a graveyard), nevertheless the whole world is, to Tom, a kind of casino. Despite Tom's pious talk of predestination, trusting in luck is, to Auden, a rejection of God: in his poem "Casino" (1936) Auden speaks of roulette-play as a kind of atheist's love-feast, "a rite of disbelief." Here Tom reveals his allegiance to the Dynamo: he abdicates responsibility for himself, lets his life be determined by mass and force.

"Come, wishes, be horses," is a common sentiment in Auden's poetry. Auden distinguishes wishes from desires—a desire is capable of being gratified, while a wish is not: "a desire for a Cadillac which may be real for a prosperous American businessman would be fantastic for a Chinese peasant" (*DH* 328). To wish—in the way that a Chinese peasant wishes for a Cadillac—is to fill oneself with self-hatred, because, as Auden explains, when the peasant asks himself why he does not have a Cadillac, the only answer is: Because I am I. The wisher ultimately wishes to be someone else. Tom's nonentity, like Faust's, springs from this fascination with alternate selves.

Hogarth, *A Rake's Progress* VI: The Gaming House

"I wish I had money" is Nick's cue to enter—he will provide the illusory identities Tom hankers for. This whole scene, from the love-duet about Aphrodite to the appearance of Nick, is an expansion of a song that Auden wrote in 1941:

> *Aphrodite's garden is*
> *A haunted region;*
> *For the very signs whereby*
> *Lovers register their vow,*
> *With a look, with a sigh,*
> *Summon to their meetings One*
> *Whose name is Legion. (CP 214)*

Here Legion goes by the name of Nick Shadow, who claims to be the servant of a recently-deceased uncle of Tom's—an uncle Tom never knew he had—who has left his fortune to his nephew. Nick urges Tom to leave the country estate and go to London to take care of business:

> *A thriving fortune has its roots of care:*
> *Attorneys crouched like gardeners to pay,*
> *Bowers of paper only seals repair . . .*
> Tom. *Well, then if Fortune sow*
> *A crop that wax and pen must cultivate,*
> *Let's fly to husbandry . . .*

The world of London banking is a mock-pastoral, growing endless reams of paper instead of fruit and foliage. This is the first appearance in the opera of the surrogate-theme, the substitution of the unnatural for the natural—a theme that will have astonishing developments in Act II. As Tom says farewell to Anne and her father, Nick steps out of character—he must show that he is not the Devil, only an actor—to announce to the audience: "The Progress of a Rake begins!"

Act I, scene 2. We are in Mother Goose's brothel. A chorus of Whores and Roaring Boys sings (in the words of the original scenario) of "the Love of War and the War of Love" (*MC* 168). Instead of inaugurating an Age of Gold, Aphrodite has joined forces with her husband Ares, not her lover Adonis; in London, sex is intimate with casual destruction. In his elegy on Freud, Auden speaks of "anarchic Aphrodite" (*CP* 218), and it is clear that the corrupt institutions of the city are not so much unnatural as themselves derived from Nature—pastoral, in a sick way. Who is more natural than Aphrodite, even when her name is Mother Goose?

Hogarth, *A Rake's Progress* I: The Heir

> Nature. *NOW WHY DID I CHOOSE*
> *TO PLAY MOTHER GOOSE?*
> *FOR MAN MY HERO IS A RAKE!*
> *YES SENIOR POET, YOU SAW THAT & MORE:*
> *SAW NATURE AS HIS PASSION AND TOO OFT HIS WHORE.*
> (The Changing Light at Sandover, *p. 485*)

In the late 1970s, the ghost of Auden (d. 1973) attended a séance at James Merrill's ouija board, and remembered with pleasure the night of the première of *The Rake's Progress*; Nature also came to the party to note that she had played the role of Mother Goose in the opera. Merrill, following supernatural instruction, put a record of the Brothel Scene onto his phonograph so that the assembled spirits could enjoy Stravinsky's music. I invite the readers of this essay to do the same, as we return to the spectacle before us.

Nick introduces Tom to Mother Goose, whom he calls the "Lady Bishop of the game." The game, of course, is chess; like Lewis Carroll's *Through the Looking-Glass*, *The Rake's Progress* is itself a kind of chess-game, where abstract figures are moved jerkily, predictably, according to rule, across a neutral field of action. Stravinsky's usual way of tackling a new assignment was to look for models; and the chief model he chose for this opera was the Mozart-da Ponte *Così fan tutte* (*All Women Do It*, 1790), a performance of which Stravinsky saw in 1948 (*PD* 72). *Così fan tutte* is an opera about two soldiers so proud of the fidelity of their fiancées, so eager to prove it to a skeptical friend, that they disguise themselves as Albanians—and each tries to seduce the other's fiancée. To their horror, both succeed, after a little struggling; but in the end the soldiers marry their original girlfriends, with fewer unrealistic expectations about the nature of love. There are some musical resemblances between Mozart's opera and Stravinsky's (*ISRP* 96; see also a review by David Hamilton, *Opus*, October, 1985, p. 25), but the most important resemblance is in the machine-tooled rigidity of the plot: either of these "heartless" operas could be staged on a chess-board, for the characters are not individuals but mathematical counters pushed through pretty symmetries of attraction and repulsion. Both operas offer strong distinctions between sexual love and the other kind: sexual love is inherently frivolous, omniform, seeking new objects, while the other kind, the love determined by vows, is stable. *The Rake's Progress* is of the eighteenth century in its niceness of categories, its plotting of its hero's progress on a grid of discriminations.

Mother Goose and Nick propound to Tom the catechism of the Dynamo:

> Nick. *What is thy duty to thyself?*
> Tom. *To shut my ears to prude and preacher*
>   *And follow Nature as my teacher. . . .*
> Mother Goose. *What is Pleasure then?*
> Tom. *The idol of all dreams, the same*
>   *Whatever shape it wear or name;*
>   *Whom flirts imagine as a hat,*
>   *Old maids believe to be a cat. . . .*
> Nick. *One final question. Love is?*
> Tom. *Love, Love!*
>   *That precious word is like a fiery coal;*
>   *It burns my lips, strikes terror to my soul.*

Here, as in the first scene, we see Tom's contempt for rules, precepts, all that restrains the free life of impulse—though, as Tom will discover, the man who chooses to be Nature's pupil is less free than he may imagine. Tom's definition of Pleasure is amusing because hat and cat seem to be such silly sources of gratification; but in fact this speech touches on one of the opera's more serious, even frightening themes, the arbitrariness of the object of desire.

We want the object of our desire to be attainable, and we want it to be dignified, culturally acceptable; but alas we crave all sorts of inappropriate and bizarre things:

> *Love requires an Object,*
> *But this varies so much,*
> *Almost, I imagine,*
>   *Anything will do:*
> *When I was a child, I*
> *Loved a pumping-engine,*
> *Thought it every bit as*
>   *Beautiful as you. (CP 207)*

This stanza from "Heavy Date" (1939)—Auden's nastiest poem—contains a message as remarkable as anything a poet ever wrote to his beloved. No one can keep his desire steadily focused: the objects of desire slip and slide grotesquely, tend to drift outside the human and the animate into broken-down industrial machines, as well as cat and hat. This is why love needs to be bound by vows: desire is too unreliable for a single night's entertainment, let alone a lifetime of companionship. Eros and Philia have nothing to do with each other, and, according to Auden, it is an error of Western civilization to pretend otherwise. "Love" is the precious word that burns Tom's lips, for he cannot find any way to integrate the Virgin, the realm of the sacred, into the secular and erotic world of the brothel. Kallman—who wrote the words of this scene—must have been thinking of Eliot's *Little Gidding* IV (1942):

> *Love is the unfamiliar Name*
> *Behind the hands that wove*
> *The intolerable shirt of flame*
> *Which human power cannot remove.*
> (Collected Poems, *p. 207)*

Stravinsky set this to music too, in a powerful four-part chorus called *Anthem* (1962).

In the brothel, a cuckoo-clock strikes one o'clock, and Tom, love-chastened, rises to leave; but Nick turns the hands back to midnight—Nick will also show himself the keeper of the opera's metronome in the graveyard scene, when he interrupts the midnight chime, gives Tom a little extra time

Hogarth, *A Rake's Progress* III: The Orgy

to sweat before carrying off his soul to hell. Tom sings to the Whores a song about the betrayal of Love, about the weeping lover who ''renews the vows he did not keep''—the Whores are saddened, moved, and offer to console him in their arms. This scene is congruent with that part of the ballet *Orpheus* in which Orpheus plays his lyre so affectingly that Hades permits him to take his dead wife back to earth—but, of course, in the Hades of the brothel, Tom is simply invited to joined the damned in their damnation. Mother Goose claims Tom as her prize for the night, and the Whores and Roaring Boys serenade them to the gayest, most light-hearted and rollicking tune in the opera:

> *The sun is bright, the grass is green.*
> *Lanterloo, lanterloo!*
> *The King is courting his young Queen.*
> *Lanterloo, lanterloo, lanterloo, my lady.*
> Women. . . . *They go a-riding. Whom do they meet?*
> Men. *Three scarecrows and a pair of feet.*
> *What will she do when they sit at table?*

Women. *Eat as much as she is able.*
   What will they do when they lie in bed? . . .
Men. *Draw his sword and chop off her head.*

Stravinsky said of these verses (written by Auden), ''I wonder whether any poet since the Elizabethans has made a composer such a beautiful gift of words for music'' (*TC* 77). But the beautiful words have some sinister suggestions. Beneath the bright excitement of Stravinsky's pseudo-Elizabethan melody, sexual love is shown to be gluttony and murder—*dying* in a sense beyond the Elizabethan one. In Act II, Tom will, in a manner of speaking, decide to marry a scarecrow—the sexual instinct seems naturally to lead to the pursuit of hollow images, ever more famishing.

In the first two scenes of Act I, we have traveled from pastoral to mock-pastoral; the mock-pastoral seems to have a real pastoral inside it (''The sun is bright, the grass is green''), yet inside this winter's-dream of spring there is only more desolation. This scene ends with Nick's summary: ''Dreams may lie, / But dream. For when you wake, you die.'' But Tom will never wake. Tom's hunger for illusory objects implicates him in fantasy more and more, and his only escape will be to the madhouse, to the endless dream-role of Adonis. There can be no exit into Nature from the competing artifices that constitute the opera.

Act I, scene 3. This brief scene consists entirely of Anne's big aria. She wonders why Tom has failed to write, and hopes that Love, and the night, and the moon can provide some sort of connective tissue between the two lovers:

> *Guide me, O moon, chastely when I depart,*
> *And warmly be the same*
> *He watches without grief or shame;*
> *It cannot, cannot be thou art*
> *A colder moon upon a colder heart.*

These lines (by Auden) show how hard it is properly to delineate the boundary between Virgin and Dynamo. Virginal Anne wants to personalize the landscape, to imbue the moon with a vague pathos, a slight warmth; but she fears that, instead, the Dynamo will infect human hearts with its own inanimation. In Auden's ''Nocturne'' (1951), the poet looks at the moon full of rapt wonder, and wishes to address the moon as ''Mother, Virgin, Muse,'' but finds that he knows too much astronomy to credit the personification:

    The Goddess, clearly, has to go,
    Whose majesty is but the mask
    That hides a faceless dynamo . . . (CP 446)

As in the opera, the subjective tenderness is a lie, and must be rejected. Stravinsky's music cleverly imitates the chill of "A colder moon upon a colder heart"; of course Stravinsky was a specialist in musical refrigeration. He once spoke of using rhythmic means to freeze the drama of Oedipus into music (*D* 29); and the freezing of *The Rake's Progress* was no difficult feat.

  Anne's aria (like the final aria of her namesake, Donna Anna in Mozart's *Don Giovanni*) ends in a great show-off cabaletta:

    Love cannot falter,
    Cannot desert;
    Though it be shunned
    Or be forgotten,
    Though it be hurt,
    If Love be love
    It will not alter.

Stravinsky has a joke at Anne's expense by making her sing rapid runs on the first syllable of *alter*—Love may not alter, but the word *alter* goes through spasm after spasm of altering. Berlioz wrote in his memoirs that he would gladly shed his own blood if he could erase the end of Donna Anna's aria, for the *roulades* destroyed the sentiment, the feeling of injury, that Mozart so carefully depicted in the aria's first section. Stravinsky, however, delights in demoting Anne from a figure of pathos to an agile soprano.

IX.

The Rake's Progress, **Act II:** Hermaphroditus

Act II, scene 1. We are back in London, where Tom is eating breakfast. The act opens with an aria of disgust:

> *Vary the song, O London, change!*
> *Disband your notes and let them range;*
> *Let rumour scream, let folly purr,*
> *Let tone desert the flatterer.*
> *Let Harmony no more obey*
> *The strident choristers of prey;*
> *Yet all your music cannot fill*
> *The gap that in my heart—is still.*
> *[recit.] O Nature, green unnatural mother,*
> *how I have followed where you led.*
> *Is it for this I left the country?*
> *No ploughman is more a slave to sun,*
> *moon, and season*
> *than a gentleman to the clock of fashion.*

This is a prayer for chaos. The previous act ended with the hope for the changeless; this act begins with the opposite request. Tom is sick of false concord, sick of hypocrisy—he wants ugliness to sound ugly. (Stravinsky's music is not ugly, but it is unsettled, slightly queasy: fragments of melodies fail to assemble into complete lines, the harmony gropes for a firm bass, the vocal ornaments seem to be embellishing nothing in particular—a pile of

57

styrofoam angels and popcorn balls without a Christmas tree in sight.) Hoping to find freedom by moving to London, Tom has instead discovered himself snared by another system, another set of rigid rules—and he is willing to go to extreme measures to extricate himself from systems.

"O Nature, green unnatural mother," though written by Kallman, is an adaptation of a line of Auden's, a line that might serve as the motto of Stravinsky's career: "Nature by nature in unnature ends." This appears in "In Sickness and in Health" (1947), a poem that deserves more than casual attention, because, in a sense, *The Rake's Progress* is a gigantic expansion of this rich lyric. It is an epithalamium, a marriage poem, ostensibly dedicated to two acquaintances of Auden's, but in fact, according to Humphrey Carpenter (*W. H. Auden: A Biography*, pp. 263, 313), the poem is a covert celebration of the vows that Auden and Kallman swore to each other. It falls neatly into two parts, Sickness and Health; or the Dynamo and the Virgin.

The Sickness section is a meditation on the precariousness of love. Love tends to decay—love is instinct with chaos. Auden looks to opera for his models of the perversions of love:

> *Nature by nature in unnature ends:*
> *Echoing each other like two waterfalls,*
> *   Tristan, Isolde, the great friends,*
> *Make passion out of passion's obstacles,*
> *Deliciously postponing their delight,*
> *Prolong frustration till it lasts all night,*
> *Then perish lest Brangaene's worldly cry*
> *Should sober their cerebral ecstasy.*
>
> *But, dying, conjure up their opposite,*
> *Don Juan, so terrified of death he hears*
> *   Each moment recommending it*
> *And knows no argument to counter theirs:*
> *Trapped in their vile affections, he must find*
> *Angels to keep him chaste; a helpless, blind*
> *Unhappy spook, he haunts the urinals,*
> *Existing solely by their miracles. (CP 247)*

Auden thought that the complementary myths of Don Giovanni and Tristan were "diseases of the Christian imagination" (*Forewords and Afterwords*, p. 25). Each myth shows how love grows twisted, incoherent, if it lacks a *telos*—a finite, intelligible object of affection. Love is confounded by an infusion of the infinite: Tristan's boundless love for Isolde reduces all the rest of the universe to zero; while Don Giovanni is in love, not with a woman, but with his list, an infinite series of conquests—"Don Giovanni's pleasure in seducing women is not sensual but arithmetical'' (*DH* 119). Stravinsky remembered that, when Auden first visited him to work on their opera, Auden talked about Tristan and Isolde (*MC* 157)—and I imagine that Auden's favorite theories on the viciousness of absolute love were discussed during the original formation of the scenario.

Stravinsky studied the score of *Don Giovanni* (1787), as well as that of the subsequent opera by Mozart and da Ponte, *Così fan tutte*, while he worked on his own; and, though Tom Rakewell is not quite so promiscuous, his affections are every bit as energetically vagrant as those of Don Giovanni. *The Rake's Progress* is a kind of sequel to *Don Giovanni*: the libertine has at last exhausted sexual delight (during the intermission between Acts I and II), reached the end of the endless list, and so decides that he must seek novel stimulation through strange, strange paths.

The Sickness section of ''In Sickness and in Health'' goes on to show that perverse sexual love is the cause of all wars—the Roaring Boys of *The Rake's Progress* were right in thinking that a good smash-up lies at the end of whoring. The Health section of ''In Sickness and in Health'' suggests the only possible cure for love-disease, the only way to confine love to a single coherent shape: the vow:

> *All chance, all love, all logic, you and I,*
> *   Exist by grace of the Absurd,*
> *And without conscious artifice we die:*
> *So, lest we manufacture in our flesh*
> *The lie of our divinity afresh,*
> *Describe round our chaotic malice now,*
> *The arbitrary circle of a vow. (CP 248)*

Anne Trulove offers Tom a means of self-definition, self-circumscription, personhood, instead of the continual refinement of sensation that Tom has sought. Distention of being, shapelessness and self-hatred fall upon Tom in the absence of Anne's control. The arbitrary vow offers relief from the natural and the unnatural alike.

Long before writing ''In Sickness and in Health,'' Auden explored the relationship between the natural and the unnatural. In a journal of 1929, Auden wrote that the unnatural is the goal of the human race:

The progress of man seems to be in a direction away from nature. The development of consciousness may be compared with the breaking away of the child from the Oedipus relation. Just as one must be weaned from one's mother, one must be weaned from the Earth Mother (Unconscious?). . . .

Man is a product of the refined disintegration of nature by time. (*The English Auden*, p. 298)

But as Auden became a Christian, he found that he could not value the un-natural—the sophisticated, the hyperconscious—any more than the natural. He continued, however, to posit a continuum between the two, even a convergence of opposites; that is why nature naturally ends in unnature. When Caliban in *The Sea and the Mirror* is made to speak like a drag-queen Henry James, it is because Nature can utter only inarticulate grunts and moans—a wholly unnatural tongue is the only way of calling attention to this central languagelessness. As Stravinsky said, Nature is only a convention, just like any other.

Tom Rakewell too cultivates the unnatural life: he eats "curious viands" and drinks the "precious wines" of Oporto and Provence until he chokes on them. It is precisely because he is Caliban, a Nature-worshiper, that he declines into such abstraction from Nature; he slides wildly from one end of the continuum to the other. Aphrodite, the goddess of Nature, has goaded Tom into an increasingly chaotic, stylized, studied, denatured way of life—fine port instead of fruit juice. Only Anne holds out the promise of escape. Tom must choose between two systems: a regulated life based on appetite (Aphrodite) or a regulated life based on a vow of love (Anne). But instead, Tom, at the behest of the Devil, tries to deny both sets of rules, both artifices, and espouse the life of radical freedom.

At the end of his aria "Vary the song," Tom exclaims "I wish I were happy." After hearing a similar whine in Act I—"I wish I had money"—Nick provided money; now he will provide some pseudo-happiness. He shows Tom a portrait of—of all people on the face of the earth—a "gorgon," a hideous circus performer, Baba the Turk, and advises Tom to marry her. Tom is aghast, but Nick explains his reasoning. He says that men are unhappy because they are unfree:

> *Why? Because the giddy multitude are driven*
> *by the unpredictable Must of their pleasures*
> *and the sober few are bound by the inflexible*
> *Ought of their duty, between which slaveries*
> *there is nothing to choose.*
> *Would you be happy? Then learn to act freely.*
> *Would you be free? Then learn to ignore*
> *Those twin tyrants of appetite and conscience.*

To marry Baba the Turk is to escape from the grid, to embrace the unpredictable.

The introduction of Baba is the crucial element in the plot of *The Rake's Progress*. In the original scenario, Tom was to marry an Ugly Duchess—exactly as in Hogarth—not a circus freak; and it would be interesting to know how Auden and Kallman came to the notion of a *mariage gratuit*. The great master of the theme of gratuitous action was André Gide, whose *Les Caves du Vatican* (1914) tells the story of a sophisticated nature-child who murders a stranger simply to prove himself free and capable of anything. A gratuitous act is a hole in the causal chain, an irruption of chaos, as Nick explains in an aria:

> *For he alone is free*
> *Who chooses what to will, and wills*
> *His choice as destiny.*
> *No eye his future can foretell,*
> *No law his past explain*
> *Whom neither Passion may compel*
> *Nor Reason can restrain.*

This speech is a paraphrase of Gabriel's Annunciation to the Virgin Mary in Auden's Christmas oratorio *For the Time Being* (1942):

> *Since Adam, being free to choose,*
> *Chose to imagine he was free*
> *To choose his own necessity,*
> *Lost in his freedom, man pursues*
> *The shadow of his images. (CP 279)*

Nick's offer of Baba the Turk is a type of the Fall of Man. The useless exercise of freedom ruined Adam—and, just as Gabriel predicts, Tom Rakewell, lost in freedom, will pursue the most farfetched images, provided by Nick Shadow.

Stravinsky's music betrays the impossibility of freedom: most of the aria advances calmly, steadily, predictably, though Nick keeps declining to sing the cadence proffered by the orchestra; in the middle, when Nick starts his chiasmus between freedom and choice, there is a sudden outburst of whistles (fossils of the whistling villain of the original scenario) in the orchestra, as if the music had at last escaped from its own pulse; but in fact the whistling figures are stiffly symmetrical, as law-determined as anything else. This musical undercutting of the libretto is somewhat like the wooden-horse episode of Richard Strauss' tone-poem *Don Quixote* (1898), in which the orchestra portrays the imaginary ride through the air in great gusts, swoops, surges of notes—but a loud pedal-point in the bass lets us know that the wooden-horse never got off the ground.

After the aria, Nick and Tom look at each other and gradually break out in loud laughter. The scene ends with a lively duet, in which Tom thinks how scandalous his marriage will be: "My tale shall be told / Both by young and by old." He is already starting to see himself as a character in a drama—he can conceive human identity only as an arbitrary role, easily shed, a prelude to his complete self-oblivion in Act III, scene 3, where he is all tale, no man.

Act II, scene 2. Anne stands uncertainly outside Tom's house. She sings an aria of resolution to screw up her courage:

> *Hear thou or not, merciful Heaven,*
> *ease thou or not my way;*
> *A love that is sworn before Thee*
> *can plunder Hell of its prey.*

Here, as elsewhere in the opera, she sounds like one of those noble, ineffectual, not too interesting Mozart characters, such as Don Ottavio in *Don Giovanni.* She is puzzled by the numerous, strange-shaped packages that servants are carrying into Tom's house. A sedan-chair enters, and Tom steps out; he dismisses her eager greetings and tells her to leave vicious London, where "Virtue is a day coquette"—real virtue has no place in it, just as Love burned a hole in the catechism of Pleasure in Act I, scene 2. Despite his protestations of unworthiness, Anne keeps insisting on his return—until a heavily veiled woman thrusts her head through the sedan-chair window and starts to reprove Tom for his poor etiquette. It is Baba the Turk, Tom's new wife; Anne's hopes are crushed. Tom, Anne, and Baba sing a trio, actually a sort of duet plus one, for Baba's impatient interjections are in a different acoustic world from the close harmonies of Anne and Tom, interechoing:

Anne. *Could it then have been known*	Tom. *It is done.*
When spring was love, and love	*I turn away, yet should*
took all our ken,	*I turn again*
That I and I alone	*The arbour would be gone*
Upon that forsworn ground	*And on the frozen ground*
Should see love dead?	*The birds lie dead.*

Baba is ceremonious, extraverted, while Tom and Anne turn inward to their private pastoral, a January eclogue. Like the Lanterloo chorus in the brothel scene, this duet suggests the nullity at the opera's heart. The pastoral is the most artificial of the modes through which nature can be represented—a landscape of decorous vegetables and toy sheep; and here it has been still further emptied of nature, until it contains little besides dead birds.

At the end of the trio, Anne flees, and Tom helps Baba out of the sedan-chair; as they advance with majestic lentor to Tom's house, Baba receives the cheers of her many admirers. At the threshold she turns to the crowd, throws open her veil to reveal a full black beard—and the scene ends.

Baba's hermaphrodite nature has always been vexatious. In 1948, Stravinsky's lawyer, one Aaron Sapiro, urged him not to compose the opera, because it would make him an accessory to the "homosexual joke of Baba the Turk" (*PD* 648)—no fool he. Stravinsky was obviously willing to take that risk, but why did Auden and Kallman introduce a bearded lady into the action?

There is some literary precedent for Baba. In Poulenc's opera *Les Mamelles de Tirésias* (*The Dugs of Tiresias*, 1947), with a libretto by Cocteau, the heroine, Thérèse, is a feminist fed up with her husband: she decides to become a man by removing her breasts from her blouse and letting them float away like balloons—and completes her transformation into Tiresias by growing a beard before our eyes. Death, too, is purely conventional: murdered characters can come back to life at the librettist's convenience. Auden spoke approvingly of Cocteau's dramatic art (*A Certain World*, p. 92) and had produced Cocteau's Orphée in 1934 (Carpenter, *WHAB* 167); it is likely that news of the just-written opera had reached him. Both Thérèse and Baba are characters that have cut themselves free from the inconveniences of fact—for them, male and female and life and death are reversible jackets, simply matters of fashion.

And yet, Baba is not entirely Dada. Insofar as she introduces an undertone (in some productions a countertenor) of submerged homosexuality into the opera, Baba derives some of her force from Auden's theories about homosexuality. Auden thought that homosexuality was more ritualized, stylized, magical than heterosexuality (*FA* 453); and, if the progress of the human race is a steady advance into the unnatural, as he said when he was young, it is also a movement toward the homosexual. Earlier in this essay I quoted two stanzas from "In Sickness and in Health" concerning Tristan and Don Giovanni, emblems of unnatural love; and in Auden's mythology both are homosexual: "the Tristan and Isolde one actually meets are a Lesbian couple, the Don Juan a pederast" (*FA* 25). As Tom Rakewell's tastes keep sophisticating away from the organic, a bearded lady starts to become the proper object of affection.

Auden's fullest published account of the nature of homosexuality occurs in his essay on J. R. Ackerley, "Papa was a Wise Old Sly-boots." Ackerley was an editor, man-of-letters, and troubled homosexual, who slept with disappointing young working-class men but who achieved lasting happiness—Auden calls it a ''miracle'' (*FA* 453)—through the love of an Alsatian bitch named Tulip. We have already seen the instability of the object of desire, how it may seek such extravagances as pumping-engines; and in Ackerley's case the object of desire mutated completely outside the human, to a lucky dog. Clearly Tulip was a more loyal and satisfying companion than Baba the Turk; but in both cases we see the exorbitance of desire, its tendency to exhaust heaven and earth and still to crave something beyond.

In Auden's view, Don Giovanni, despite his frenzy to hug every woman (or boy) alive, is secretly a man who wants nothing at all:

> The man who refuses to be the servant of any *telos* can [not be represented in a drama]. He can sing his rapture of freedom and indifference, but after that there is nothing for him to do but be quiet. In a drama he can only be represented indirectly as a man with a *telos*, indeed a monomania, but of such a kind that it is clear that it is an arbitrary choice; nothing in his nature imposes it on him or biases him toward it. Such is Don Giovanni. (*DH* 118-19)

Such also is Tom Rakewell. Auden takes the fact that Don Giovanni does not care whether his conquests are rich or poor or ugly or beautiful as a sign of the arbitrariness of his affection. Baba the Turk is a personification of arbitrariness; Auden does not have to show Tom engaging in multiple seductions precisely because Baba is all of Don Giovanni's conquests rolled into one. Tom seems to have unlimited desires; but in fact he is no one and desires nothing. Baba is simply Nothing, made embraceable.

Act II, scene 3. This begins with a sample of Tom's married life: breakfast with Baba:

> As I was saying, both brothers wore moustaches,
> But Sir John was taller; they gave me the musical glasses.
> That was in Vienna, no, it must have been in Milan
> Because of the donkeys. Vienna was the Chinese fan
> —or was it the bottle of water from the River Jordan?
> I'm certain at least it was Vienna and Lord Gordon. . . .
> You're not eating, my love. Count Moldau gave me the gnome,
> And Prince Oblowsky the little statues of the Twelve
>   Apostles,
> Which I like best of all my treasures except my fossils.
> Which reminds me I must tell Bridget never to touch the
>   mummies,
> I'll dust them myself. She can do the waxwork dummies.
> Of course, I like my birds, too, especially my Great Auk.

This is a patter-song, but strangely shrill and emphatic—Gilbert and Sullivan in hell. In fact the whole musical atmosphere has been shifting during Act II. The music of Act I had something of the settled character of a textbook of old musical forms—or, more exactly, approximations to and witty evasions of old musical forms. Perhaps in imitation of Alban Berg, Stravinsky decorated his published score with form-labels (not just Aria and Recitative, but Cavatina, Cabaletta, Duet-Finale, and so forth). But in this scene the music is more modish; some of the music that Stravinsky wrote for Baba sounds slightly like Poulenc—busy, breezy, chattery, full of false gestures, as if the emotional suggestions were to be put in quotation marks. Baba's breathless barrage of detached sixteenth-notes has an almost inhuman speed—it is machine-music; and Baba is herself (to borrow the title of a Klee painting) a twittering machine. Tom has married the robot that was the last and greatest of Casanova's loves in Fellini's film.

Baba is the mechanical bird of *The Nightingale* promoted into the semblance of human shape. The singing-contest of the earlier opera appears intact in *The Rake's Progress*, for Anne Trulove is a reincarnation of the ''real'' nightingale, mooning over the countryside and embodying an ideal of warmth and purity of expression. Once again a hero is asked to choose between the real and the mechanical; once again we see the jealousy, the intimacy that exists between them.

Why would Stravinsky conceive Baba as a sort of wind-up toy? In many ways, Baba signifies something exactly opposite to a machine: she embodies randomness, freedom—she is an object of desire chosen by a cast of dice, herself in love with the miscellaneous. But it is hard to make a convincing musical representation of disorder, and I think that Stravinsky had good reason to treat Baba as he did.

Several times Stravinsky faced the problem of trying to find the shape of shapelessness, to make something artistic out of the random. In his card-

game ballet "in three deals," *Jeu de Cartes* (1937), "The Joker [the principal dancer] is a bonus, an element of chance and an escape from . . . combinations" (*TC* 45); but the music that characterizes the Joker offers no striking contrast to the (not very good) music of the rest of the ballet. In the television operacule *The Flood* (1962), Stravinsky (like Haydn in *Die Schöpfung* [*The Creation*, 1798]) wanted to write a prelude to represent chaos, but found the task puzzling:

> How, please, does one represent chaos in music? I took certain elements, intervals, and chords made up of fourths. My "material of Chaos" is limited, however, and I couldn't make my Chaos last very long. (*ED* 124)

Baba is the Joker in the card-game of *The Rake's Progress*, and the Chaos in its version of the Fall of Man—and Stravinsky found a better way of realizing her character than in the other two cases. Stravinsky (especially if he had written the opera in the 1960s) might have wondered for a moment whether to have her sing something like aleatory music, music in which the notes are determined by random processes—throwing dice, notating the pattern of raisins in a fruitcake or birds on telephone wires. But Stravinsky hated this sort of music. Among the milder of his many denunciations of aleatory music is this:

> What I cannot follow are the manic-depressive fluctuations from total control to no control, from the serialization of all elements to chance. (*TC* 33)

Here is a clue about the musical formation of Baba: Stravinsky has rebounded from no control (what Baba represents) to total control. Just as Auden leaped from goallessness to an arbitrary goal in inventing her, so Stravinsky leaped from the stochastic to the all-determined in writing the proper music for her. Like Offenbach's Olympia in *Les Contes d'Hoffmann*, Baba sings music that sounds at times like a singer's practice-exercises, lalálalalálalalá.

Unlike Olympia's aria (which speaks of little but pretty birds singing prettily in the trees), Baba's songs have a wide field of reference—from the River Jordan to the North Pole. She is a collector of knickknacks from all over the world, and she likes to talk about them, admire them. She is surrounded by things, emphatically dead things: fossils, mummies, waxwork dummies—the triumph here is the Great Auk, which manages not only to be flightless and stuffed but extinct. They seem to infect her with their thingliness, make her seem even more frantically inert than before. As she babbles on—her very name seems to suggest Babel—she seems puzzled by

Tom's boredom; she cannot understand any human emotion except the lust for objects, the lust to become an object.

Soon Baba grows angry at Tom, and assumes that he is distracted by thoughts of Anne; she storms about, smashing objects—objects alone can be her means of emotional relief. As she starts exercising her chest-register on the first syllable of "never," Tom rises suddenly, seizes his wig (in the original scenario a tea-cosy), and plops it down on her head; she stops in mid-note, freezes, and remains for the rest of the scene in this strange mock rigor mortis. The gorgon is herself turned to stone. She has become a backwards Petrushka, cast by magic into the form of a doll.

Tom falls asleep after this "murder"; and Nick enters, wheeling in with him a "fantastic baroque machine." He puts a loaf of bread in one compartment, and a piece of broken china into the machine's hopper; by turning a wheel he makes the loaf fall out of a chute. It is the most obvious sort of fraud. This pantomime of wheeling and cranking is accompanied by nonchalant piccolo whistles.

Since this scene began we have watched two "transformations": a woman has been turned to stone, and a stone has been turned into bread. Of course, each is only a parody of a transformation: Baba is still Baba, and the stone is still a stone. Perhaps the character of *The Rake's Progress* is clearer in this scene than anywhere else: musically and dramatically it is an opera of non-transformations.

A history of opera could be written on the theme of metamorphosis. In eighteenth-century opera, metamorphosis is conducted mostly through stage-machinery, not through music; even in a forward-looking opera like Gluck's *Armide* (1777), the great finale, during which demons raze Armide's palace and the sorceress flies away in a rage, is accompanied by a pleasant racket in the orchestra—but it is brief and fairly static, a representation of the horror aroused by the transformation, not of the transformation itself. One of the great achievements of nineteenth-century opera was the invention of persuasive musical representations of change: in Wagner's *Parsifal* (1882), for example, the second act ends with the spectacle of a magic castle falling into dust; but the musical figure that represents the collapse is not simply stated and repeated, Gluck-fashion, but spun out over many bars,

(Tom rises suddenly, seizes his wig and plumps it down over her head, back to front, cutting her run off.)
(*Tom steht plötzlich auf, nimmt seine Perücke und stülpt sie ihr, ihre Kadenz abschneidend, mit der Rückseite nach vorne über den Kopf.*)

moving lower and lower in pitch, as bits of rubble bounce in lower and lower arcs, a nightmare of ruin.

In *The Rake's Progress*, we have music that declines the privilege of metamorphosis. As Paul Griffiths notes in his helpful book on the opera, ''Stravinsky does not modulate but rather slips from one key into another'' (*ISRP* 99). *The Rake's Progress* is formally jagged, like Matisse's scissor-cut stars and waves glued onto a background, instead of the imperceptible graduation of tone in oil painting. Stravinsky juxtaposes keys in such a way as to leave them unrelated to each other, instead of painstakingly demonstrating the relation. I believe that Stravinsky's theory of Nature is behind this practice: for Wagnerian metamorphosis assumes that an artificial form must be slowly, carefully undone, transformed into its natural form—a given *leitmotiv* can be tricked up in a thousand pretty ways, but each variant is measurably deviant from an original; Stravinskian non-metamorphosis, on the other hand, assumes that one form, or figure, or key, or system of organizing musical ideas, is no more natural or just than any other. What sets Stravinsky apart from the eighteenth- and nineteenth-century opera composers is that Auden's and Kallman's text calls for mock metamorphoses, not real ones; the plot and the music agree.

While Nick demonstrates his hoax to the audience, Tom dreams; and when Tom awakes he tells Nick his dream, of a marvellous machine that can make ''earth become an Eden of goodwill.'' Nick whips the dust cloth off the contraption—there it is. Here Nick asserts his character as a corrupt Ariel: he stands for false imagination, a faculty that will enmire Tom more and more deeply in flimsy unrealities. In this appeal to fantastic ambition, Nick is also the well-known Satan of Genesis, as Auden's plot outline shows:

Bordel	—Le plaisir [Pleasure].
Baba	—L'acte gratuit [The gratuitous act].
La Machine	—Il désire devenir Dieu [He wishes to become God].

(*MC* 161)

As Tom, the mock god, plans his recapture of Paradise he takes a giant step into unnature—accompanied by a sprung, spangled, bearded Eve. In a duet, Tom, ''très exalté,'' exclaims over his wondrous machine, while Nick invites the audience to buy shares in the company that will market it: ''there's no fantastic lie / You cannot make men swallow if you try.''

X.

The Rake's Progress, Act III: The Marriage of Heaven and Hell

Act III, scene 1. The Auction Scene. Instead of the heaven on earth predicted in the last scene, we open with cries of "Ruin, Disaster, Shame." The bubble of speculation has burst: duchesses have committed suicide, orphans forage in the street, and all the goods of bankrupt Tom are to be auctioned. Anne is looking for Tom, but no one knows where to find him. The babblers come to order as Sellem, the auctioneer, mounts his dais. Sellem makes large claims about the existential value of auctions:

> *Truly there is a divine balance in Nature:*
> *a thousand lose that a thousand may gain;*
> *and you who are the fortunate are not so*
> *only in yourselves, but also in being Nature's*
> *missionaries. You are her instruments for the*
> *restoration of that order we all so worship,*
> *and it is granted to, ah! so few of us to*
> *serve.*

Like the roulette wheel in Auden's "Casino," the auction is an instrument for one of the sacred rites of the Dynamo: the random redistribution of objects. Nature is a zero-sum game, and Sellem is the priest who celebrates the equation of profit and loss. In Act II we ventured into the far reaches of the unnatural; in Act III, many sorts of artifices and illusions will be scattered, dispelled, as Nature's equilibrium is restored once again. In the Stravinsky canon, Sellem's role is that of Namer, like the square-dance caller in *The*

Flood who enumerates the animals in Noah's Ark; to the heap of vendable objects—as disconnected, as lacking in syntax, as those in the bags toted around by the mute pedants of Swift's Lagado—Sellem provides a corresponding heap of words.

Sellem is overcome by a strange glee in the performance of his rite: amid exclamations of La! and Hmmm! and Poof! he sells a mounted fish and a Roman bust—each item leading to surge of arithmetical excitement in the crowd, as bids are shouted. It is an illustration of the Dynamo's essentially numerical nature. For his third item, Sellem walks up to the covered Baba:

> *An unknown object draws us, draws us near.*
> *A cake? An organ? Golden Apple Tree? . . .*
> *Oracle? Pillar? Octopus? Who'll see?*
> *Be brave! Perhaps an angel will appear.*
> *La! come bid.*
> *Hmmm! come buy.*
> *Aha! The it.*

Baba is the algebraic x, an all-purpose thing, a representation of the mutability of the object of desire. She seems about to decompose into a whole hardware store or museum basement. When Sellem calls her "The it," there may be an allusion to one of Auden's favorite books, Georg Groddeck's *Das Buch vom Es* (*The Book of the It*, 1923), which describes an impersonal evolutionary force (the It), a drive that directs the growth of all life on earth through its confused attempts to realize itself. Auden identified the It with Aphrodite, the sexual instinct; and Sellem's strange comment may therefore be a clue about the unity of Baba and Aphrodite, Unnature and Nature. It is as if, at the end of the evolution of life on our planet, Aphrodite would grow a beard and a mainspring.

After Baba is sold, Sellem snatches Tom's wig from her head; this ends her suspended animation, and she resumes singing "never" at the exact point she left off in Act II, scene 3. Like the murdered characters in *Les Mamelles de Tirésias*, Baba can come back to life at any time—she is a piece of nonsense, beyond the usual constraints of life. She does not understand that time has passed, and thinks that thieves are trying to loot her apartment.

Outside, the voices of Nick and Tom are heard, singing a street-vendor's chant: "Old wives for sale!" Clearly dispossession has not dampened their spirits; and Baba too soon reconciles herself to the loss of her gnomes and apostles and mummies and all the rest. Anne enters, and the crowd settles down to watch what it hopes will be a still more interesting event than the auction: the confrontation of Baba and Anne. But instead of recriminations,

Baba offers Anne some unexpected advice: Go find Tom, for he still loves you. In Act III there are a great many reversions from the unnatural to the natural, but this is perhaps the most surprising of all: Baba evolves from a thing into a person. Under Anne's—the Virgin's—benevolent gaze, even the Dynamo can grow kind, develop a human face. Sellem wondered whether an angel might lie underneath Baba's dust-cover; and for a moment it seems that he was right.

As Baba imperiously announces her imminent return to the stage, Tom and Nick are again heard singing outside the window:

> *If boys had wings and girls had stings*
> *And gold fell from the sky,*
> *If new-laid eggs wore wooden legs*
> *I should not laugh or cry.*

Anne recognizes Tom's voice and runs after him. This sour careless rhyme shows how far the rake has progressed into disillusionment since we saw him in Act II, scene 3, about to market his stone-transformer, his machine to get gold from the sky. Preposterous dreams will trouble Tom no longer— he will not laugh or cry. Nick, in the next scene, will no longer be Ariel, the conjurer of fantasies, but instead the punishing destroyer of fantasy.

Act III, scene 2. The Graveyard Scene. The prelude to this scene was the first music Stravinsky wrote for the opera, and it is perhaps the most frigid music he ever wrote—the temperature is well below the chilliest moment of Puccini's *La Bohème* (1896) Act III, or of Vivaldi's Winter concerto (1725), or of the winter masque in Purcell's *King Arthur* (1691). Nick and Tom are alone. A year and a day (the stated period of the contract) have passed, and Nick claims his wage: Tom's soul. Instead of the infinite fancies of Act II, Tom in Act III is in a domain of strict terms and precise obligations. Nick points to the open grave that awaits Tom, and takes several objects out of his bag: a knife, a rope, a bottle of poison, a gun. Tom's options, once amazingly wide-ranging, have contracted to these: a choice of means for suicide. Nick's bag contains an even less attractive assortment of objects than Baba's apartmentful of knickknacks. In Act II Tom married a thing; now he is himself in danger of being reified.

As the ninth chime sounds on the approach to fatal midnight, Nick agrees to stop time and play a card game for Tom's soul: if Tom can guess the three cards Nick pulls out, Tom is saved. For the first card, Tom guesses the Queen of Hearts—a symbol of Anne. That is correct. For the second card, Tom is stymied:

> Tom. . . . *how throw the die*
> *To win my soul back for myself?*
> Nick. *Was Fortune not your mistress once?*
> *Be fair.*
> *Give her at least the second chance to bare*
> *The hand of Shadow.*
> *(The spade suddenly falls forward with a great crash.)*
> Tom. (startled, cursing) *The deuce!*
> *(He looks at what fell.) She lights the shades*
> *And shows the two of spades.*

Nick asks whether Fortune has been Tom's mistress. She has, in Act II, in the person of Baba, the random object of desire; but in this scene Tom's mistress is not Fortune but Love, Anne Trulove. It is Love that leads Tom to rationalize, to find design in random events—such as a spade's sudden tumble. A card game, even more than a chess game, is a pure exercise in mathematical fortuity, an investigation of the patterns of disordered things—that is why Lewis Carroll wrote *Alice's Adventures in Wonderland* (1865), his playing-card fable, before *Through the Looking-Glass* (1871). Up to now Tom has flirted with Disorder, perhaps even slept with her; but now he is trying to align his wishes, his hope of survival, with some principle of Order. Following appetite has led Tom further and further into the waste land, until he is now at the brink of the grave; his last hope is to find some other system on which to base his life.

Of course that guess is correct, too. For the last card, Nick decides to play a trick: he slips the discarded Queen of Hearts back into the pack, and selects it as the final test. With mounting horror, Tom sees the track of cloven hooves, feels damnation near. But at the last minute he hears Anne, singing a phrase from her aria in Act II, scene 2:

> *A love*
> *That is sworn before Thee can plunder*
> *Hell of its prey.*

This phrase is sung with no bar lines, as if it were absolute, a pure cantilation outside the meter of the rest of the opera. Here Anne offers Tom a real

telos, a finite, intelligible goal for his affection—in great contrast to the chimerae that drove him on throughout the first two acts. Tom guesses the Queen of Hearts once again, and is saved. Nick's contract was not the only one Tom agreed to; his vows to Anne also constituted a contract, much violated but still in force. In ''In Sickness and in Health,'' the arbitrary vow of love can ''show the whirlwind how to be an arm'' (*CP* 248), can rescue from chaos and constitute a firm image of self and other. Similarly Anne's vow can force the distended Tom back into human shape.

Tom is saved, but his sins enable Nick to punish him by taking away his reason; and Nick sinks into the grave intended for Tom:

> *I burn! I burn! I freeze! In shame I hear*
> *My famished legions roar;*
> *My own delay cost me my prey*
> *And damns me all the more.*

This great cry is accompanied by the most ferocious music in the score, as if sledgehammers were driving Nick into the ground—the rhythmic force is somewhat similar to that of certain Verdi arias, such as *Eri tu* in *Un Ballo in Maschera* (1859). For the first time we see (or, more exactly, hear) Nick for what he is: Satan—the music is worthy of his majesty. *The Rake's Progress* is an opera full of secrets and disguises, but not metamorphoses: Nick and Anne and Baba and the rest have an underlying allegorical significance, from which only slight deviations are permissible. The function of the music is to keep steady focus on the value of each figure: clearly to denominate Nick as Ace of Spades, Anne as Queen of Hearts, Baba as Joker.

The scene ends with mad Tom smiling in the dawn, transfigured: ''Adonis is my name.'' His reversion to Nature is now complete, for he is both a fertility god and a Natural in the archaic sense of the word—an idiot.

He has explored all of Unnature and turned upside-down in the concave mirror once again. He is hauled off to the lunatic asylum.

Act III, scene 3. The Madhouse Scene. Bedlam is populated with figures directly from Hogarth: a crippled soldier, a man with a telescope, a blind man with a broken fiddle—this last madman appealed to Stravinsky from the beginning (*MC* 155), and suggests the ruin of music, the falling-into-discord that Tom requested at the beginning of Act II, scene 2. Tom answers to no name but Adonis, and insists that his fellow madmen are also ''heroic shades'':

> *Anoint your limbs with oil,*
> *put on your wedding garments . . .*
> *Venus, queen of Love, will visit*
> *her unworthy Adonis.*
> Madmen. *Madmen's words are all untrue;*
> *She will never come to you.*
> Tom. *She gave me her promise.*
> Madmen. *Madness cancels every vow . . .*

Hogarth, *A Rake's Progress* VII: The Madhouse

But vows are stronger than the madmen suppose. To some extent the madmen are willing to participate in Tom's fantasy—for example, they refer to their Keeper as Minos, the judge of dead souls. But for the most part the madmen understand that Bedlam is a realm where there are no identities, mythological or social or otherwise:

> *Down in Hell as up in Heaven*
> *No hands are in marriage given,*
> *Nor is honour or degree*
> *Known in our society.*
> *Banker, beggar, whore and wit*
> *In a common darkness sit.*

(This chorus is an adaptation of Auden's "Domesday Song" of 1941:

> *Jumbled in one common box*
> *Of their dark stupidity,*
> *Orchid, swan, and Caesar lie . . . [CP 213]*

Most of Tom's career has been a cultivation of non-being, a striving after the random; and Bedlam is the logical culmination, a chamber of clouds, a heat-sink of identity, a condition of complete freedom.

Anne comes, and Tom invites his Venus to mount her throne. Anne is not Aphrodite but the Heavenly Venus, Urania—also the Muse of Astronomy, as the madman's telescope might hint. Tom confesses to her that he has been caught "In a foolish dream," and has "hunted shadows"—he asks her forgiveness. The shadows that he renounces include not only Nick Shadow but all the false Venuses—Mother Goose (sexual indulgence), Baba (gratuitous action), Fortune—that had lured him into the waste land. In the midst of despair comes grace—Auden was a Kierkegaardian, and *The Rake's Progress* is, among many other things, a parable of Fear and Trembling. Anne in the madhouse operates as a clandestine Holy Ghost. Auden liked to scandalize less adventuresome Christians by announcing that heavenly grace was arbitrary—and that too is illustrated in the opera's magnificent celebration of the Arbitrary.

Anne has succeeded in making a heaven of hell: "Rejoice, beloved: in these fields of Elysium / Space cannot alter, nor time our love abate." The Rake's Progress is at last coming to a halt—his progress never was much more than the frantic illusion of change. As Anne and Tom embrace, they assume the same posture they had in Act I, scene 1, as if the opera had never happened at all, as if Baba and Nick and all the rest were indeed nothing but foolish dreams. Within the arbitrary circle of a vow Anne and Tom are immune from phantoms.

Tom is weary, and asks Venus to sing him to sleep. Anne responds with our century's most ravishing lullaby:

> Orchards greenly grace
> That undisturbéd place,
> The weary soul recalling
> To slumber and to dream,
> While many a stream
> Falls, falls, falls,
> Descanting on a child-like theme.
> Madmen. O sacred music of the spheres!

She sings of the Islands of the Blest, and of the Peaceable Kingdom where the lion and the lamb are friends. Her vision of pastoral resembles some of the more frigid pastorals seen in the earlier acts; but the touches of the sacred, of a child's picture-book of heaven, place it on a different plane of artifice. The speaking landscape is Auden's favorite image of paradise—indeed, he once wrote that the first sign to Adam and Eve of the Fall was that "The stream was dumb with whom they'd always planned" (CP 150). Here that stream is re-voiced. At the end of The Sea and the Mirror, Caliban tells us that Shakespeare included Caliban in order deliberately to spoil the beauty of his play, and, furthermore, that a Christian poet should always try to botch his best effects, to include in his work a shock of disillusion—for in the unbridgeable gap between ideal and real the vision of grace, the prefigurement of heaven, must constitute itself. The Rake's Progress has insisted on its illusory character in many ways—through the asides to the audience, through the presentation of absurd, unassimilable, indigestible characters like Baba; the opera discredits itself from beginning to end. And amid the general collapse, Anne's lullaby hints at a revelation beyond fiction.

Anne can do no more for Tom, and so leaves—as her father says, "the tale is ended." Tom awakes, finds her missing, and calls on Achilles, Helen, Eurydice, Orpheus, Persephone—the madmen—to show where they have hidden her. But she is gone.

> Tom. My heart breaks.
> I feel the chill of death's approaching wing.
> Orpheus, strike from thy lyre
> a swanlike music,
> and weep, ye nymphs and shepherds

of these Stygian fields,
weep for Adonis, the beautiful, the young;
weep for Adonis whom Venus loved.

And he dies. The summoning of Orpheus may have awakened in Stravinsky a memory of the aria *Possente spirto* from Monteverdi's *Orfeo* (1607)—the aria in which Orpheus tries to charm implacable Charon into letting him enter Hades—for Stravinsky's vocal line is nearly as florid and expertly mournful as Monteverdi's. Much of the character of this final declamation comes from a musical device, a rapid quavering up and down a half-tone interval, which we hear at "Stygian fields," "the beautiful, the young," and "Venus loved"—as if Tom's voice were breaking with emotion, and had to end each phrase with a catch in his throat. Similar figures have been heard elsewhere in this scene: during Tom's and Anne's duet, we hear the same quick flickers all through "Rejoice, beloved: in these fields of Elysium / Space cannot alter, nor time our love abate."

Elsewhere in Stravinsky's late works, we find crucial lines decorated with this same figure: for example, in the second of his *Three Songs from William Shakespeare* (1953), the whole song is a continual tissue of these half-tone shakes:

Full fadom five thy Father lies,
Of his bones are Corrall made:
Those are pearles that were his eies,
Nothing of him that doth fade,
But doth suffer a Sea-change
Into something rich and strange . . .

Stravinsky himself called attention to his use of a different but related figure: in his *Elegy for J.F.K* (1964)—his only setting of an Auden text besides *The Rake's Progress*—Stravinsky used (at the line "The heavens are silent") a rising and falling whole-tone interval, slightly slower and wider than the figure I have been speaking of. He called this two-note chain "a recurring stutter in my musical speech from as long ago as *Les Noces*" (*TC*

61). Not long afterward Stravinsky wrote *Introitus: T. S. Eliot in Memoriam* (1965), in which "The music of '*et perpetua*' is a quotation of my setting of Auden's line 'The Heavens are silent' " (*TC* 66).

Why should the same, or similar, music be used to describe the timelessness of Elysium, the sea-change of King Alonso into coral and pearls, and the deaths of John F. Kennedy, Tom Rakewell, and Tom Eliot? It is clearly the figure that Stravinsky uses to mean immortality. On one hand, it is the quake of a man overcome with feeling; on the other hand, it is simply a blank oscillation of pitch, without direction, without any particular impulse of melody or harmony or rhythm—change so pointless that its embodies unchangingness. It lies at the place where the expressive touches the inexpressive, where bone starts to turn into coral, where life is at the edge of death. (Strangely enough, Christopher Hogwood has pointed out that Handel has an immortality-motive, also a rising and falling whole-tone phrase, used in *Messiah* [1742] and *Acis and Galatea* [1718].) Stravinsky's music cannot illustrate metamorphosis, because it constitutes itself in a boundary-region where there is no distinction to be made between nature and artifice, eye and pearl, expression and its opposite.

Many of Stravinsky's works end with what Stravinsky called an apotheosis: a passage of solemn repetitions of a short phrase, slowly intensifying and dissolving. To such music, in *Apollo*, the god assumes his godhead; in *Orpheus*, the lyre lives on though the hero dies. *The Rake's Progress* does not have a declared apotheosis, but the Madhouse scene ends with a lament for Adonis, a sternly lugubrious chorus that takes the place of an apotheosis. Tom is deified, though in a less happy manner than Apollo. Both the apotheosis and the immortality-figure are means by which Stravinsky's music declares its essentially static nature. Often in his later years he commented on this quality of standing-still: "my later music is . . . static and objective" (*D* 124). I think this is why Stravinsky wanted to write an opera in which all the action is imaginary, all the expression histrionic: he needed a plot that stood still.

the hea-vens are si-lent

Epilogue. This brief conclusion, like the Graveyard scene, is an adaptation of an idea prominent in *Don Giovanni*. The characters, wigless and beardless, comment on their own theatricality, offer little fragments of moral advice:

> Anne. *Not every rake is rescued*
> *At the last by Love and Beauty;*
> *Not every man is given an Anne*
> *To take the place of Duty. . . .*
> Tom. *Beware, young men who fancy*
> *You are Virgil or Julius Caesar,*
> *Lest when you wake*
> *You be only a rake. . . .*
> All. *. . . For idle hands*
> *And hearts and minds*
> *The Devil finds*
> *A work to do . . .*

Anne's message is a version of one of Auden's favorite endings, that of Brecht's *Die Dreigroschenoper* (1928), where a messenger rides up to the gallows, as the thief Macheath is about to hang, and announces that the queen has spared his life and given him a castle; and Mrs. Peachum notes how good life would be if messengers always appeared in such fashion. In other words, the fable is deceptive. Tom tells us, on the other hand, to take the fable seriously. Not every critic has thought that Auden intended us to take the final proverb—the devil finds work for idle hands—as the true moral of the opera. But it is an opera that shows how mankind is corrupted either by infinite goals (to be Virgil or Julius Caesar, to restore paradise) or by the absence of goals (idleness)—so perhaps the moral is surprisingly just.

Through this essay we have seen many convergences of opposites: nightingale and machine, chaos and total control, nature and artifice. Robert Craft has told us that, in the late 1930s, when Stravinsky was preparing notes to help Roland-Manuel write *Poetics of Music*, Stravinsky read Nicholas of Cusa and became interested in the notion of *coincidentia oppositorum* (*SC* II 503). Nicholas of Cusa was a fifteenth-century German prelate, whose best-known treatise is called *De Possest* (*Of Can-Is*, or *On Actualized-possibility*). Stravinsky probably took note of this passage:

> And when we attempted to see Him beyond being and not-being, we were unable to understand how He could be visible. For He is beyond everything simple and everything composite, beyond everything singular and everything

plural, beyond every limit and all unlimitedness; He is completely everywhere and not at all anywhere; He is of every form and of no form, alike; He is completely ineffable; in all things He is all things, in nothing He is nothing . . . He is encountered—unlike any other existing thing—ignorantly or unintelligibly, in a shadow or in darkness or unknowingly. . . . [He is encountered] as a thing in which opposites coincide (e.g., motion and rest, together)—not as two but as above duality or otherness. This vision occurs in darkness, where the hidden God is concealed from the eyes of all the wise. (*De Possest* 74, in Jasper Hopkins, *A Concise Introduction to the Philosophy of Nicholas of Cusa*, pp. 151, 153)

Human thought is bound by dichotomies; but God refuses to be limited by such divisions. Elsewhere Nicholas of Cusa offered the following exercise for imagining God: consider a child's top; the faster it spins the stabler it becomes; if it were spinning infinitely fast, it would be at rest. God is at the coinciding-point of motion and rest.

If God were to be embodied in music, how could it be done? Stravinsky was a pious man, and wrote a number of liturgical settings and psalms; and I think that *The Rake's Progress* is also about God. Through the coincidence of opposites, he made oblique reference to the hidden God of Nicholas of Cusa, ineffable, dwelling in darkness. Indeed, Stravinsky contemplated a coincidence of opposites that would have horrified Nicholas: the coincidence of God and the Devil. We read among his working-notes to *The Flood*: "God's music is sometimes reminiscent of Shadow's music in *The Rake*, which should prove, if proof were needed, that musical identities are purely circumstantial" (*D* 73). Similarly (indeed to my ear more noticeably), the hen-scratching tune of Nick's first speech, "Fair lady, gracious gentlemen," is a faster version of the main melody of the second movement of the *Symphony in Three Movements* (1946), a piece written to illustrate Bernadette's vision of the Virgin Mary for a film of Werfel's *Song of Bernadette*.

Stravinsky liked these consternating reversals because they showed the arbitrariness of the link between music and its meaning or reference; but he also may have enjoyed them because, by intensifying music's ineffability, they provided an intuition of the divine, beyond human conceptions of good and evil. *The Rake's Progress* has little in common with the other great opera of our age, Schoenberg's *Moses und Aron* (1932); and yet it is possible to believe that each gropes after an expression of the inexpressible, an image of what cannot be confined to an image. The inexpressive and the inexpressible may turn out to be one and the same. Yeats once spoke of a friend who dreamed of God in the form of a slug, as if what is "beyond comprehension is mirrored in the least organized forms of life" (*A Vision*, p. 284). But Stravinsky, like Kleist, preferred to represent God by means of even lower forms, by nonsense-syllables and painted dolls.

INDEX OF WORKS BY STRAVINSKY MENTIONED IN THE TEXT

BIBLIOGRAPHY OF WORKS CITED IN THE TEXT

W. H. Auden, *A Certain World: A Commonplace Book* (New York: Random House, 1970).

CP   W. H. Auden, *Collected Poems*, ed. Edward Mendelson (New York: Random House, 1976).

DH   W. H. Auden, *The Dyer's Hand and Other Essays* (New York: Random House, 1962).

W. H. Auden, *The English Auden: Poems, Essays, and Dramatic Writings, 1927-1939*, ed. Edward Mendelson (New York: Random House, 1977).

FA   W. H. Auden, *Forewords and Afterwords* (New York: Random House, 1973).

WHAB   Humphrey Carpenter, *W. H. Auden: A Biography* (Boston: Houghton Mifflin, 1981).

T. S. Eliot, *Collected Poems, 1909-1962* (New York: Harcourt Brace, 1963).

Lyndall Gordon, *Eliot's Early Years* (Oxford: Oxford University Press, 1977).

ISRP   Paul Griffiths, *Igor Stravinsky: The Rake's Progress* (Cambridge: Cambridge University Press, 1982).

SR   Ethan Haimo and Paul Johnson, eds., *Stravinsky Retrospectives* (Lincoln: University of Nebraska Press, 1987).

MAD   Mathias Hansen, ed., *Arbeitsheft 35: Musikalische Analyse in der Diskussion / Gespräche, Analysen, Dokumentation* (Berlin: Akademie der Künste der Deutschen Demokratischen Republik, 1982), pp. 50-63.

E. T. A. Hoffmann, *Weird Tales*, trans. J. T. Bealby (Freeport, N.Y.: Books for Libraries Press, 1970).

Jasper Hopkins, *A Concise Introduction to the Philosophy of Nicholas of Cusa* (Minneapolis: University of Minnesota Press, 1980).

Heinrich von Kleist, *An Abyss Too Deep: Letters of Heinrich von Kleist with a Selection of Essays and Anecdotes*, ed., trans., and intro. by Philip B. Miller (New York: E. P. Dutton, 1982).

Minna Lederman, ed., *Stravinsky in the Theatre* (New York: Da Capo Press, 1975).

James Merrill, *The Changing Light at Sandover* (New York: Atheneum, 1983).

Thomas Pynchon, *V.* (New York: Bantam Books, 1968).

David Simpson, *Fetishism and Imagination* (Baltimore: Johns Hopkins University Press, 1982).

R. Stephan, ed., *Über Musik und Sprache* (Mainz: Schott, 1974).

A   Igor Stravinsky, *An Autobiography* (New York: W. W. Norton, 1962). This is an anonymous translation of *Chroniques de ma vie* (1934).

SC   Igor Stravinsky, *Selected Correspondence*, volume II, ed. Robert Craft (New York: Knopf, 1984).

C   Igor Stravinsky and Robert Craft, *Conversations with Igor Stravin-sky* (Berkeley: University of California Press, 1980).

D   Igor Stravinsky and Robert Craft, *Dialogues* (Berkeley: University of California Press, 1982).

ED   Igor Stravinsky and Robert Craft, *Expositions and Developments* (Berkeley: University of California Press, 1981).

MC   Igor Stravinsky and Robert Craft, *Memories and Commentaries* (Berkeley: University of California Press, 1981).

TC   Igor Stravinsky and Robert Craft, *Themes and Conclusions* (Berkeley: University of California Press, 1982).

PD   Vera Stravinsky and Robert Craft, *Stravinsky in Pictures and Documents* (New York: Simon and Schuster, 1978).

W. B. Yeats, *The Variorum Edition of the Poems of W. B. Yeats*, ed. Peter Allt and Russell K. Alspach (New York: Macmillan, 1968).

W. B. Yeats, *A Vision* (New York: Macmillan, 1956).